MEL BAY PRESENTS

Cello Method

by Christine Watts

NEW & REVISED EDITION!

Cover photo: Knilling Strad DeMunck Model 159.
Provided courtesy of Knilling String Instruments,
A Division of St. Louis Music Inc.
www.knilling.com

1 2 3 4 5 6 7 8 9 0

Visit us on the Web at www.melbay.com — E-mail us at email@melbay.com

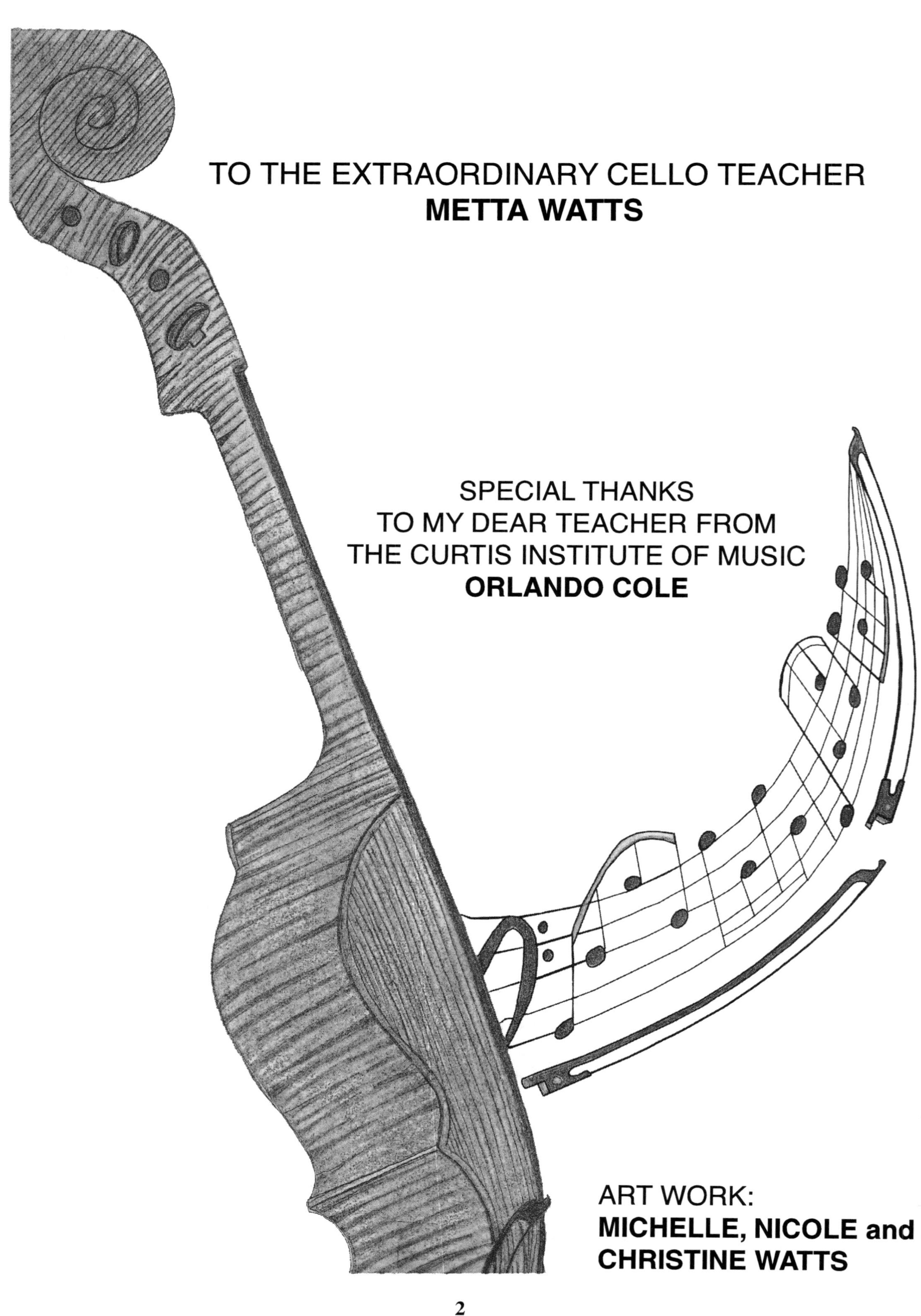

TO THE EXTRAORDINARY CELLO TEACHER
METTA WATTS

SPECIAL THANKS
TO MY DEAR TEACHER FROM
THE CURTIS INSTITUTE OF MUSIC
ORLANDO COLE

ART WORK:
MICHELLE, NICOLE and CHRISTINE WATTS

Table of Contents

Table of Contents 3
Introduction to cello and bow 7
Cello parts 8
Bow parts 9
How to sit at the cello 10
How to hold your bow 11
Blank staves 12
Introduction to playing the cello 13
Using your bow 14
Your bow and your sound 15
Using your wrist wisely 16
Training your ears and controlling your bow 17
Musical Alphabet, Bass Clef, Names of the Strings 18
Time Signature, Key Signature 19
Staff Names of Lines 20
Staff names of the spaces 21
Whole and Half Notes 22
Quarter and Eighth Notes 23
Bow exercises 24
Open string duets 25
Play every finger on every string 26
USING YOUR LEFT HAND 27
A string 28
D string 30
G string 32
C string 34
Songs everyone loves, Bowing Exercises, Dotted notes, The slur 37
Twinkle Twinkle Little Star 38
French song 39
Old Mac Donald 40
Elephants and Mud Song 41
Finger exercises 42
Finger exercises rules 43

EXERCISE FOR BOW CONTROL AND CELLO SOUND 44
Birds in a Tree Looking Down at Me 45
Bowing Exercises 46
Polar Bears 47
Ode to Joy, Pachelbel Canon 48
Country Dance, Humpty Dumpty 49
THE SLUR 50
The slur, Long Long Ago 51
Now We will Dance, Dancers in the Sun 52
Haydn's Surprise, Walking Song, Running Song 53
I'm a Little Tea Pot, Hot Cross Buns 54
Song of the Wind 55
Bean the Basset Hound, Waltz of the Cellos 56
Sing Little Robbin, The Cuckoo, Brahm's Lullaby 57
EXERCISE For Bow Control and Cello Sound 59
Finger exercise 60
March in D, Duet I 61
Duet, Simple Gifts 62
Ladybugs, The Magic Ring, Allegro 63
Morning Mood, Country fair Day 64
Hush Little Baby 65
DOTTED NOTES 66
Dotted Note Etude, Camptown Races 67
Oh Come Little Children, She'll be Coming Around the Mountain 68
Song for Lucky, Oh Susannah 69
Between the Ox and the Grey Donkey, Driedel 70
March in G 71
Turkey in the Straw, Arkansas Traveler 72
More Songs, Dynamics, Sevick Bowing, Etudes, and Duets 73
Dynamics 75
Triplets, Come Dance with Me, Irish Washerwoman 76
Triplet Etude 77
March of the Toy Soldiers 78
Soldier's March 79
The Little Fiddle, Evening Song 80

Bach Minuet in C 81
FINGER EXERCISES 82
Octaves, Etude, and Etude in C 83
Etudes 84
Bingo and Do Your Ears Hang Down? 85
Seraglio 86
My Pony, The Blue Bells of Scotland 87
EXERCISE For Bow Control and Cello Sound 88
PIZZACATO 90
Pop Goes the Weasel 91
Dotzaur Adagio 92
Flemish song, Dotzaur Duet 93
Freedom Song 94
Bach Musette 95
THE TIE, Beautiful dreamer 96
Laughing Song, Brahms First Symphony 97
BEATING YOUR FOOT 98
STRETCH POSITION FOR FLATS 100
Stretch position exercises 101
Stretch position exercises 102
Stretch position exercises 103
Teddy has Balloons, Little Flower, Blues In C 104
Ocean Fog, Wind, Monkeys in the Trees 105
Kreutzer Etude 106
Minuet 107
STRETCH POSITION FOR SHARPS 109
Stretch position exercises 110
Stretch position exercises 111
Stretch position exercises 112
Stretch position exercises 113
Stretch position exercises 114
Up and Down, Chinese Melody, Swabian Folk Dance 115
REVIEW OF EXTENDED POSITION 116
Review of extended position 117
Blank staves 118

CHANGING POSITIONS 119
Small shifts position 1-4 120
Second position 121
Third position 122
Fourth position 123
Blank staves 124
MAJOR SCALES, ARPEGGIOS AND EXERCISES 125
Scales to 3 sharps and flats 126
C major scale, Arpeggio and exercises 127
G major scale, Arpeggio and exercise 128
F major scale, Arpeggio and exercises 129
D major scale, Arpeggio and exercise 130
B♭ major scale, Arpeggio and exercises 131
A major scale, Arpeggio and exercise 132
E♭ major scale, Arpeggio and exercises 133
Blank staves 134
HOLIDAY SONGS (HALLOWEEN AND CHRISTMAS) 135
Halloween, Spirits of Halloween 137
Jingle Bells, Good King Wenceslas 138
We Wish you a Merry Christmas, O Come all Ye Faithful 139
Jolly Old St. Nicholas, Angels we have Heard on High 140
The First Noel, Up on a Roof Top 141
CONCERT PIECES 143
Minuet in C, Bach 144
Hunters Chorus, Von Weber 145
Theme from Rosamunde, Schubert 146
Quadraille, Mozart 147
Chorus form Judas Macabaeus, Handel 148
Polka, Kuffner 149
Contra Dance, Mozart 150
Petite Gavotte, Lorenzetti 151

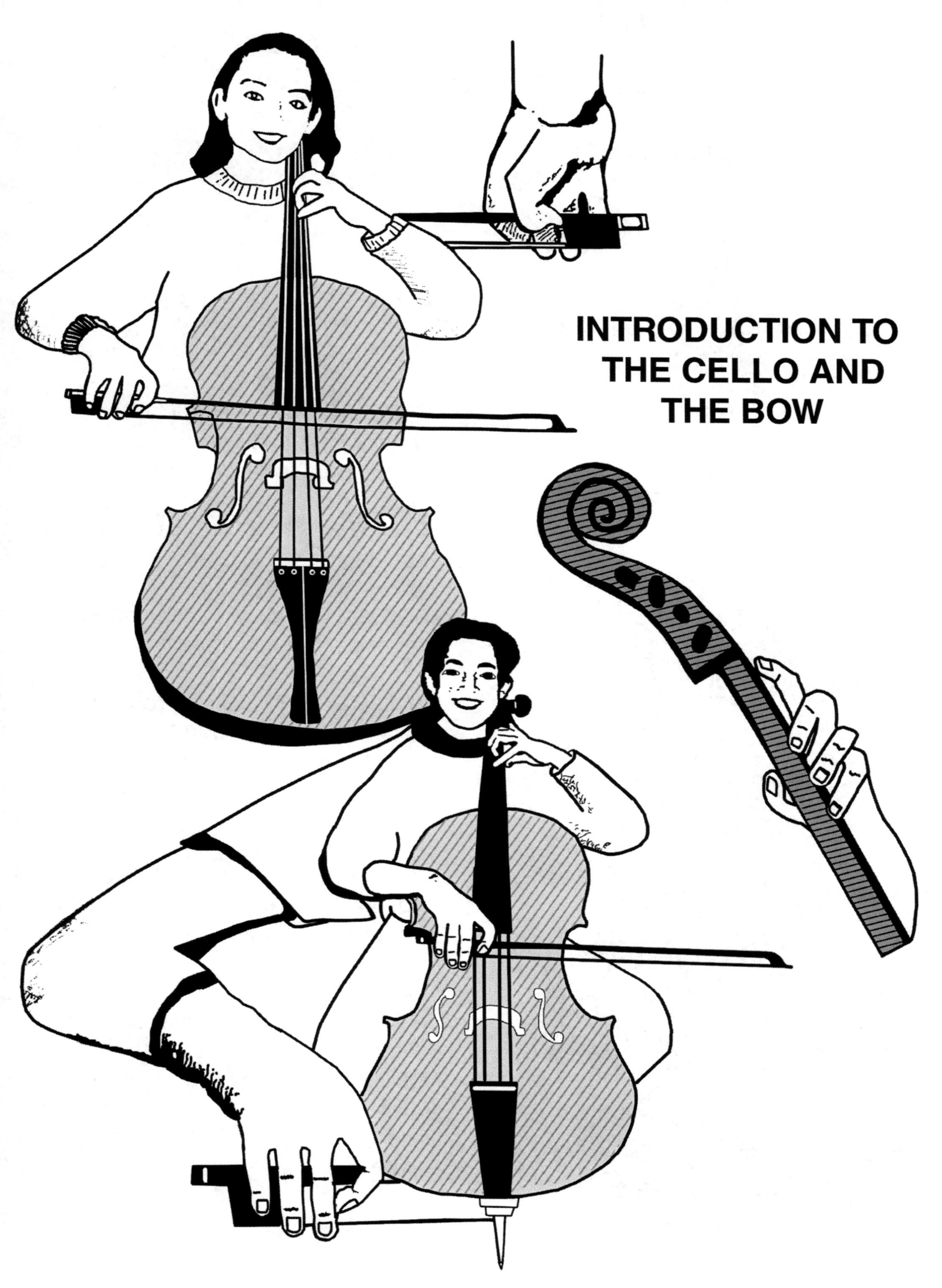

INTRODUCTION TO THE CELLO AND THE BOW

A FINE CELLO IS A GREAT WORK OF ART. IT IS BOTH BEAUTIFUL TO LOOK AT AND BEAUTIFUL TO LISTEN TO.

A cello's parts are somewhat similar to ours. There is a "head, neck, body and leg."

SCROLL: The cello's "head".

NECK: Runs from head to body.

FINGERBOARD: The long thin piece of wood with strings on top where you put your fingers to make notes.

A D G C The four strings from highest to lowest.

BRIDGE: Holds the strings up just like the ones that hold roads up.

SOUND POST: A narrow cylinder of wood under the bridge which carries sound from the back to the front of the cello. You can see it if you look through the *f* holes.

***f* HOLES:** Are sort of F shaped openings on either side of the bridge that sound comes out of.

TAIL PIECE: Narrow piece of wood which holds the strings and fine tuners.

FINE TUNERS: Screws that you turn to raise or lower the pitch of the strings a little bit. They are at the top of the tail piece.

TUNING PEGS: Big nobs on the head of the cello which are used for tuning.

A BEAUTIFUL AND WELL BALANCED BOW IS A GREAT WORK OF ART

Deep in the heart of the South American Rainforest grows the Pernambuco tree. The wood from the Pernambuco tree is strong and very flexible, which makes it perfect for cello bows.

STICK: Is the wood of the bow. It is carved from the wood of the Pernambuco Tree.

HAIR: Is cut from a horse's actual tail. Yes, it is a real horses actual hair and no, it doesn't hurt the horse at all. Their hair grows back just like yours. Some say horses are proud to have their hair used by musicians.

TIP: Is the pointy end of the bow farthest from your hand.

FROG: Is a rectangle at the end of your bow which is almost always black. The name comes from an old French word and has nothing to do with the little green animal who hops around.

ADJUSTING SCREW: Is at the frog end of the bow and is used to tighten or loosen the bow hair.

ROSIN: Hard sticky tree sap you rub on the bow hair to cause the friction which produces the sound.

CARE/USE: To use a bow you have to tighten the hairs, but not too much. The bow stick should still be curved when you are done. Before putting the bow away, loosen the hairs again.

HOW TO SIT AT THE CELLO

SIT DOWN ON A STRAIGHT BACK CHAIR and put your **FEET FLAT ON THE GROUND.** If you are extra small use an extra small chair.

PUT THE END PIN OUT 6 OR 8 INCHES. You have to try sitting with the cello before you know exactly how far. Then put the **CELLO BETWEEN YOUR KNEES.**

HUG THE CELLO IN CLOSE. Let it touch your heart. Your neck and the cello's neck almost touch. Slant the cello slightly to your right.

HOW TO HOLD YOUR BOW

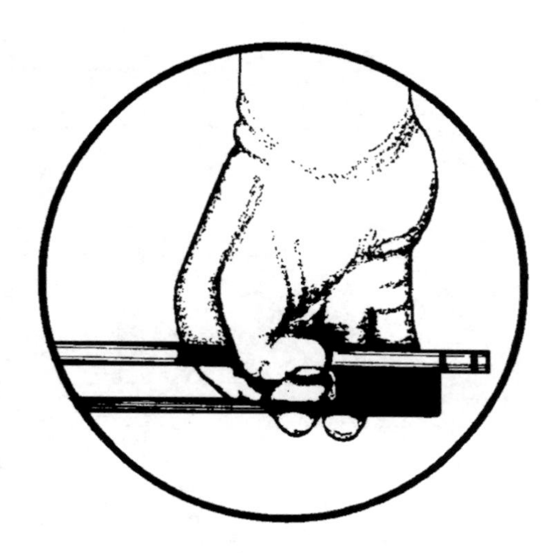

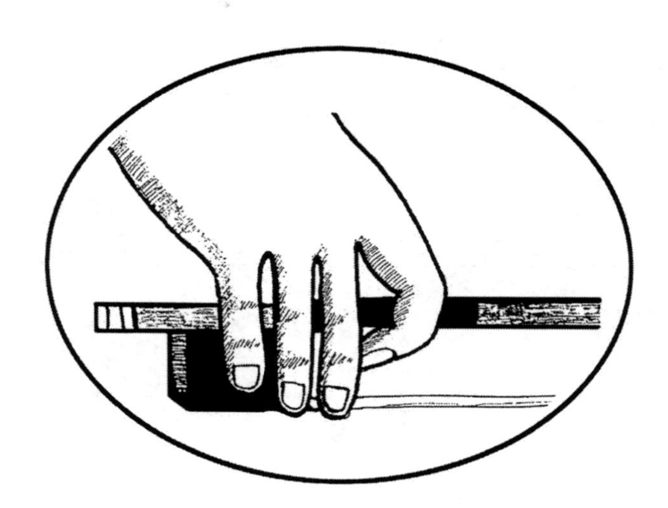

PINKY: Tip of pinky on the middle of the frog. If you have a dot put the tip of your pinky there. If not, you can use a sticker.

FIRST FINGER: First finger wrapped around the bow. Reach your first finger out a comfortable distance and then at the first joint wrap it around the bow.

MIDDLE FINGERS: Hang straight down. Let your middle fingers hang loosely down between the others. It doesn't matter if they touch the hair.

THUMB: Bent out across from 2nd finger. Look at the corner where your nail stops and your skin begins. Take that corner and put it on the side of your bow across from your 2nd finger. Make sure you put your thumb up high enough so it won't slip thru when you play. Bend your thumb out and point the joint towards the tip of your bow.

INTRODUCTION TO PLAYING THE CELLO

USING YOUR BOW

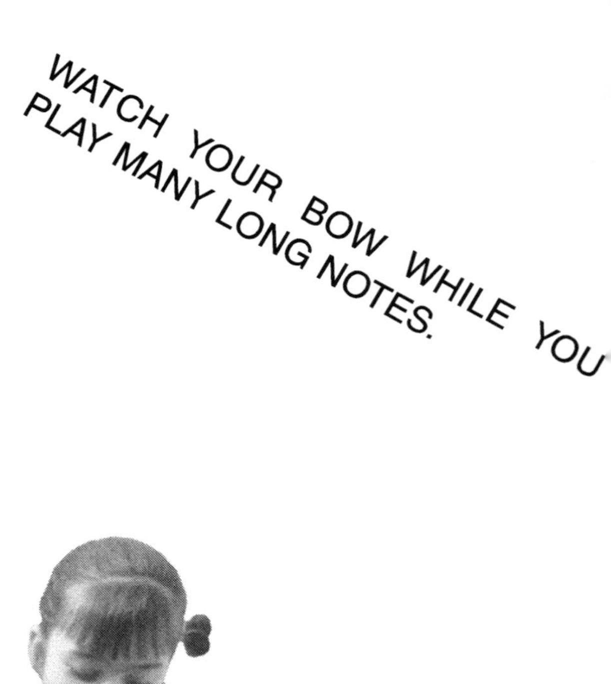

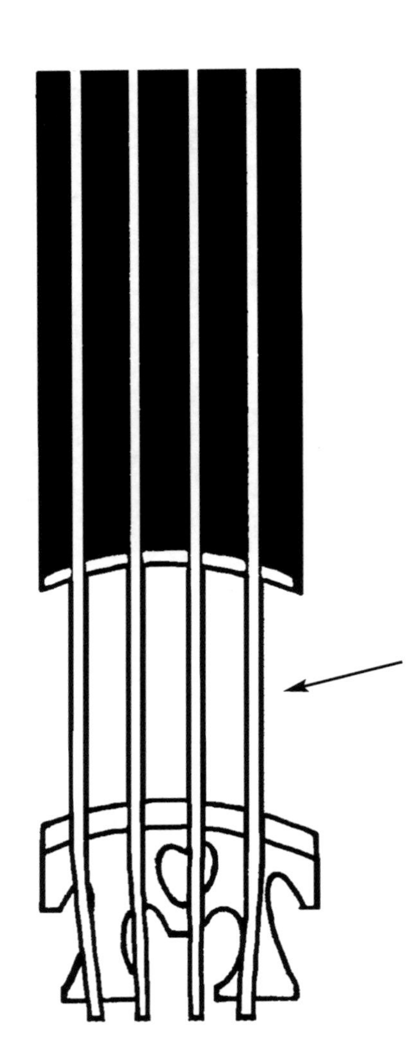

In the beginning, you should bow here, about ½ way between the fingerboard and the bridge.

Use the muscles of your shoulder wrist, arm and hand to move your bow back and forth.

DON'T BOW TOO CLOSE TO THE BRIDGE, OR YOU WILL MAKE AN UGLY SOUND.

YOU, YOUR BOW, AND MAKING A GOOD SOUND

You create every sound your bow makes. That is why, from your brain to your arm to your bow you need to be in complete control. Your brain has to tell your arm exactly what to do with your bow for each note.

1. Lean on your bow just hard enough to make a clear sound.
2. If you lean too hard you will make an ugly choking sound.
3. If you don't lean hard enough you will make a fuzzy sound.
4. You need to lean a little harder in the upper half just to maintain the same volume as in the lower half of your bow.

CHANGING BOW DIRECTION

Keep your right hand and arm steady as you carefully change the direction your bow is going in. This control is necessary to keep from making unwanted sounds as you change direction. The idea is to be able to produce a continuously beautiful sound. Keep your eyes on your bow and bow hand to make sure they are doing the right thing.

USING YOUR WRIST WISELY

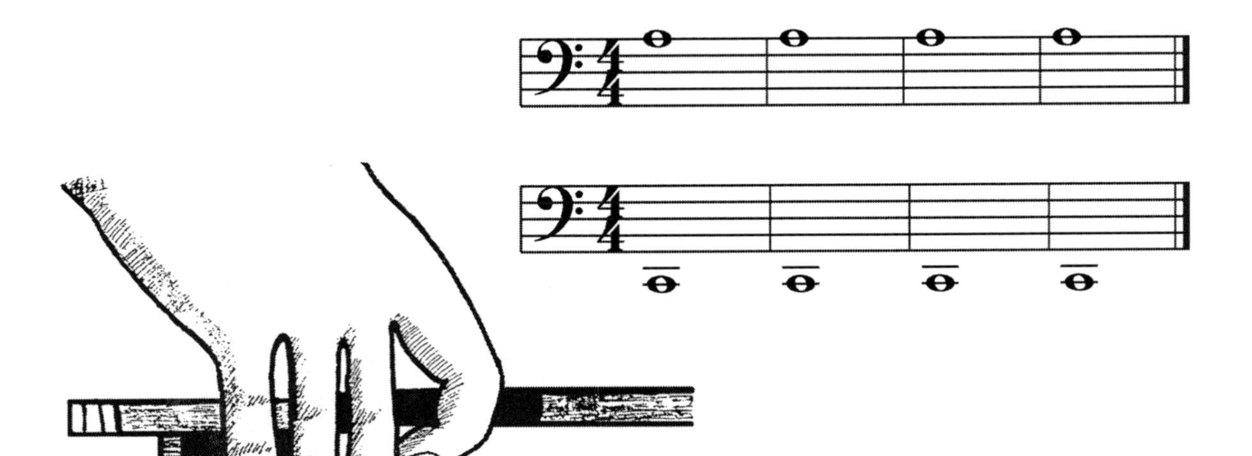

WRIST IN

Your bow must move in a straight line between the bridge and the fingerboard. You can do this by bending your wrist out on the down bows and in on the up bows.

WATCH your wrist. WATCH your bow. WATCH your arm. WATCH your bridge.

GO BACK AND FORTH MANY TIMES.
FEEL YOUR WRIST GO IN AND OUT.
WATCH YOUR BOW STAY STRAIGHT.
WHAT DOES IT FEEL LIKE?

TRAINING YOUR EARS AND CONTROLLING YOUR BOW

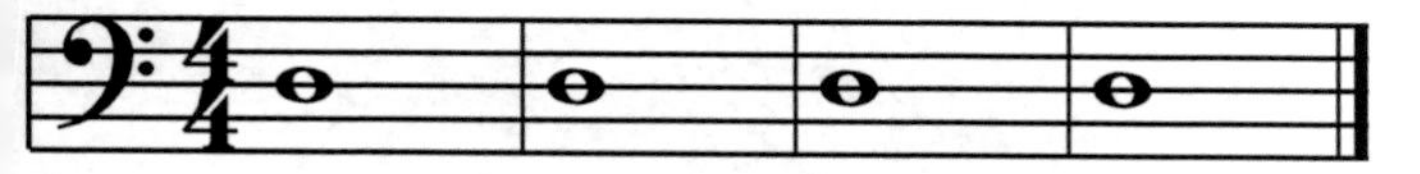

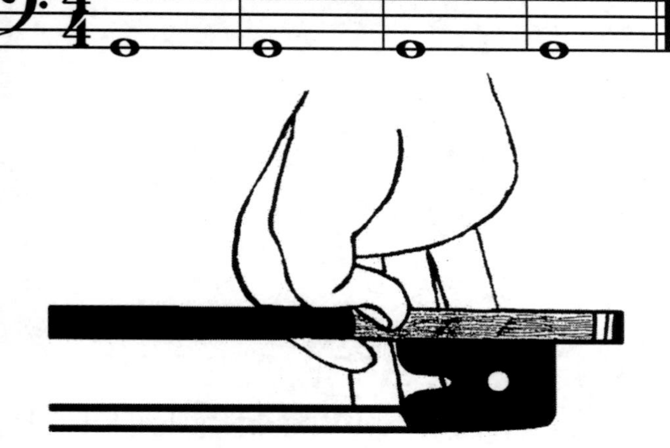

FOCUS: CAREFULLY TRAIN YOUR EARS TO LISTEN CLOSELY AND HEAR THE SOUNDS YOU ARE MAKING.

FOCUS: You are making the sounds with your bow. Can you figure out why the bow is making a good or a bad sound and fix it?

THE SOUND IS VERY DIFFERENT IF YOU BOW

1. CLOSE TO THE FINGERBOARD
2. CLOSE TO THE BRIDGE, OR
3. IN THE MIDDLE BETWEEN THE TWO.

TRY THIS TEST: Two long bows, three different sounds, keep everything the same, but play in three different places

1. Play very close to the bridge.
2. Play very close to the finger board.
3. Play in the middle between the two.

MUSIC HAS A LANGUAGE ALL IT'S OWN. IT IS WRITTEN ON FIVE LINES AND FOUR SPACES CALLED THE STAFF.

The musical alphabet is short. It goes from A to G then it starts over again with A.

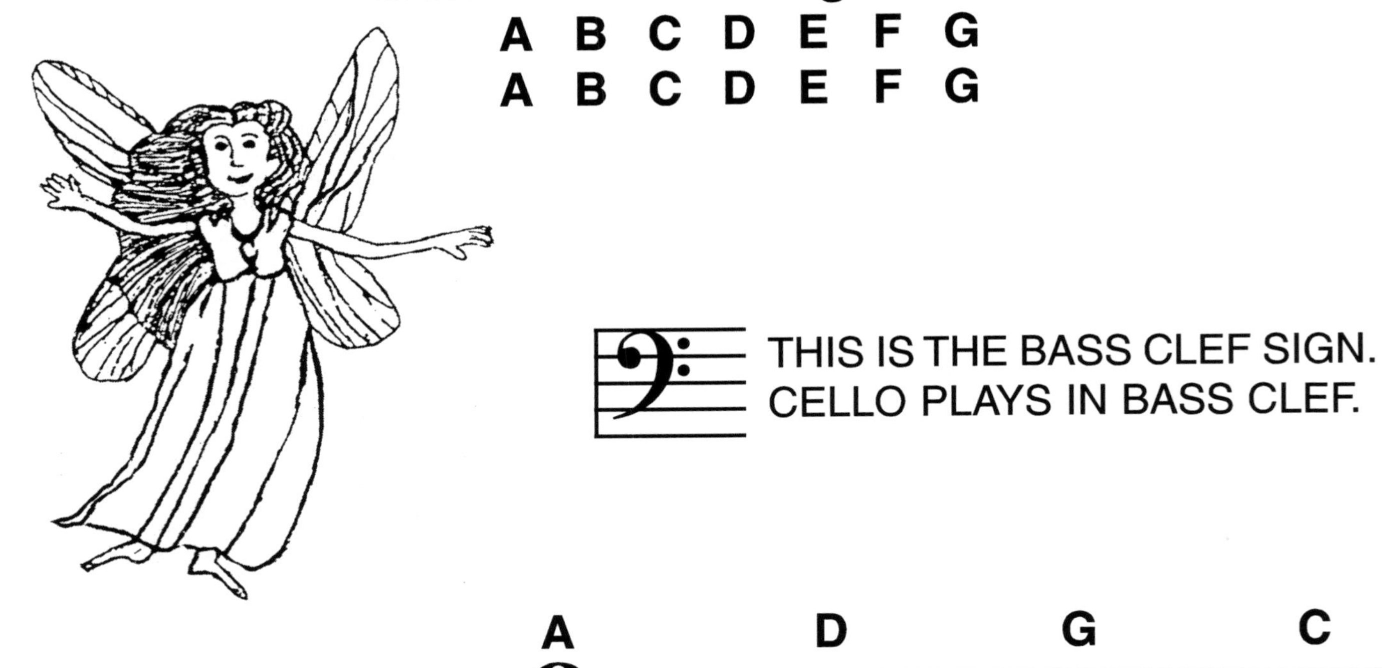

A B C D E F G
A B C D E F G

THIS IS THE BASS CLEF SIGN.
CELLO PLAYS IN BASS CLEF.

A D G C

THE CELLO HAS 4 STRINGS.
Memorize the names of the cello strings as soon as you can.
Memorize where they are on the staff.

A STRING	TOP LINE OF THE STAFF
D STRING	MIDDLE LINE OF THE STAFF
G STRING	BOTTOM LINE OF THE STAFF
C STRING	TWO LINES BELOW THE STAFF

TIME SIGNATURE

A TIME SIGNATURE LOOKS LIKE A FRACTION EXCEPT THERE IS NO LINE BETWEEN THE NUMBERS. IT IS RIGHT AFTER THE CLEF SIGN.

TOP NUMBER = HOW MANY BEATS IN A MEASURE

BOTTOM NUMBER = WHAT KIND OF NOTE GETS A BEAT

KEY SIGNATURE

THE KEY SIGNATURE TELLS US HOW MANY FLATS OR SHARPS ARE IN A PIECE OF MUSIC.

At the beginning of a piece of music with the clef sign and the time signature comes the KEY SIGNATURE.

F♯ is ALWAYS the first sharp.
B♭ is ALWAYS the first flat.

THE STAFF HAS 5 LINES

You also add lines below and above the staff as needed.

GOOD BUNNIES DANCE FAST AWAY

Each word in this sentence starts with the name of a line.
Just for fun, make up a sentence of your own in which
each word starts with the name of a line.

G B D F A

_ _

Now write a row of notes on each line.
Say out loud where the note is as you write it.

G is the bottom line

B is the first line up

D is the middle line

F is the fourth line up

A is the top line

THE STAFF HAS 4 SPACES

You also add more spaces above or below as needed.

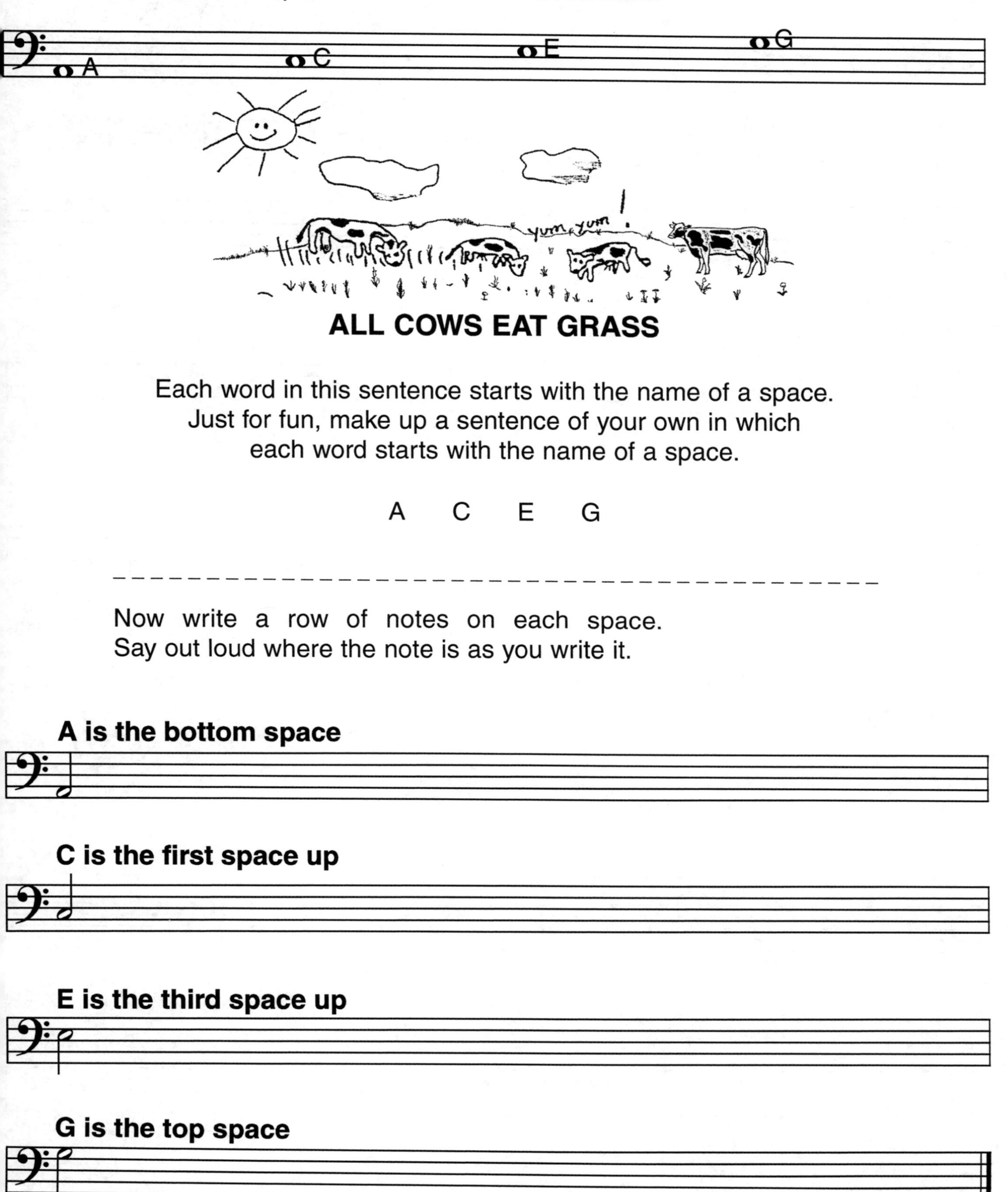

ALL COWS EAT GRASS

Each word in this sentence starts with the name of a space.
Just for fun, make up a sentence of your own in which
each word starts with the name of a space.

A C E G

_ _

Now write a row of notes on each space.
Say out loud where the note is as you write it.

A is the bottom space

C is the first space up

E is the third space up

G is the top space

WHOLE NOTES

Whole note = 4 beats of sound
Whole note rest = 4 beats of silence

HALF NOTES

Half note = 2 beats of sound
Half note rest = 2 beats of silence

TO THE TOP OF THE HILL AND DOWN AGAIN

Know what kind of note you are playing.

QUARTER NOTES

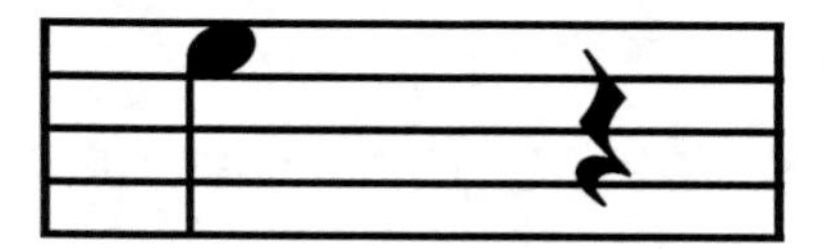

Quarter note = 1 beat of sound
Quarter note rest = 1 beat of silence

EIGHTH NOTES

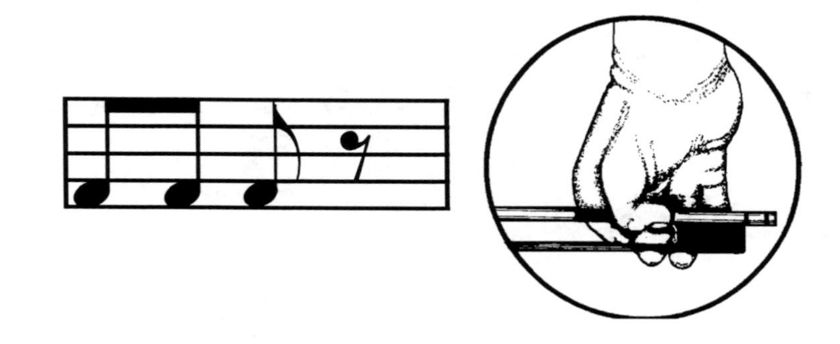

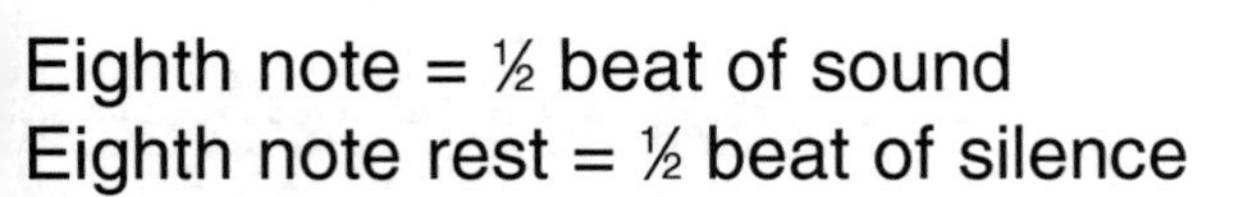

Eighth note = ½ beat of sound
Eighth note rest = ½ beat of silence

BOW EXERCISES

Practice changing strings without making any extra noises.
It takes control and practice to touch only one string at a time.
Hold your bow firmly and move your arm carefully.
Keep the motion smooth and relaxed.

Everyone has to figure out for themselves exactly
how far to move their arm to get their
bow exactly where it needs to be.
How big you are, the curve of your bridge,
and the exact size of your cello
make the choice yours.

WATCH AND FEEL YOUR BOW ARM
AS IT LIFTS AND LOWERS THE BOW

OPEN STRING DUETS

$\begin{matrix}3\\4\end{matrix}$ REVIEW: In the time signature, what does the top number mean, and what does the bottom number tell you?

RAINFOREST

OLD GREEN TREES

RAIN DROPS FALLING ON LEAVES

USING YOUR FINGERS TO PLAY THE NOTES

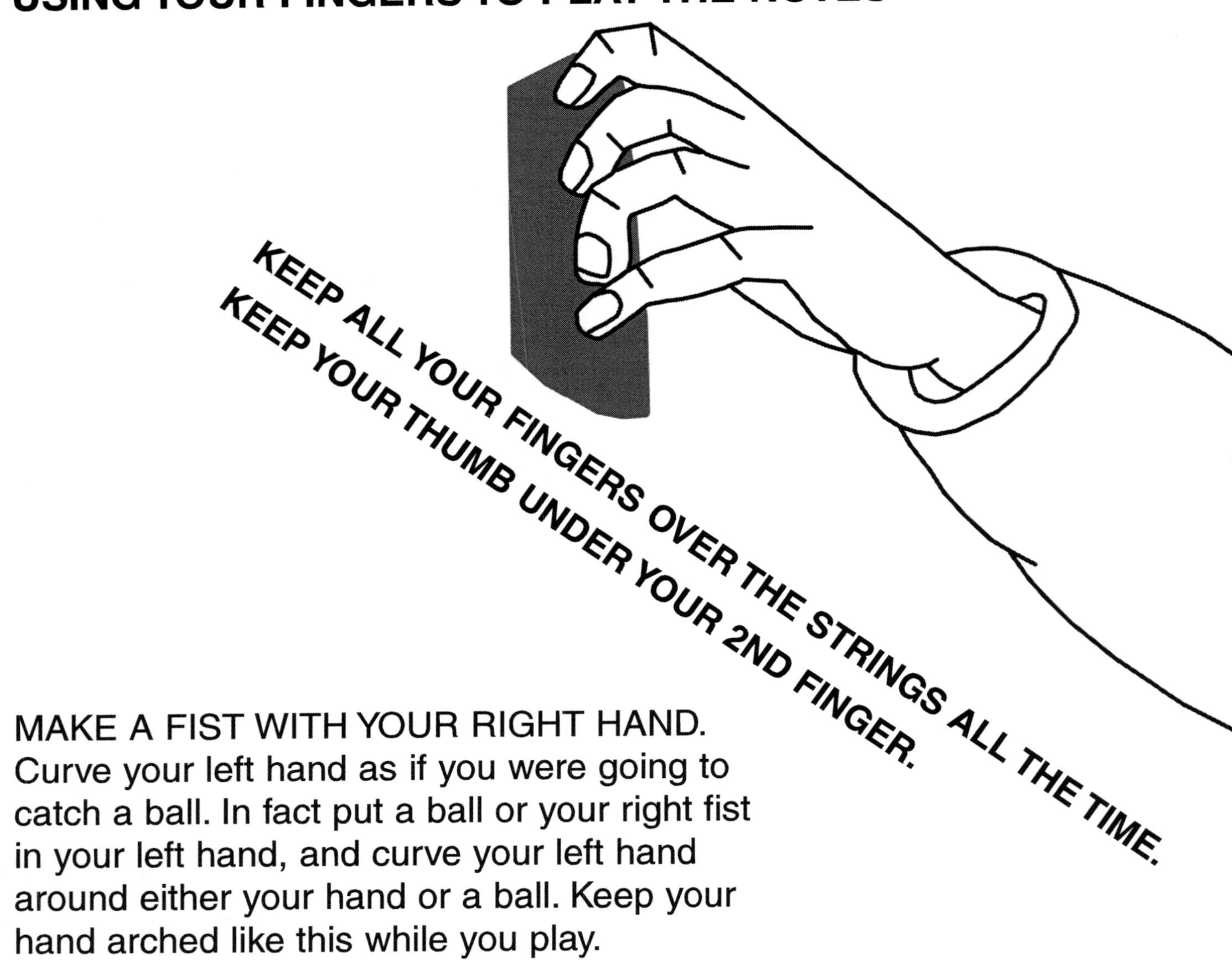

MAKE A FIST WITH YOUR RIGHT HAND. Curve your left hand as if you were going to catch a ball. In fact put a ball or your right fist in your left hand, and curve your left hand around either your hand or a ball. Keep your hand arched like this while you play.

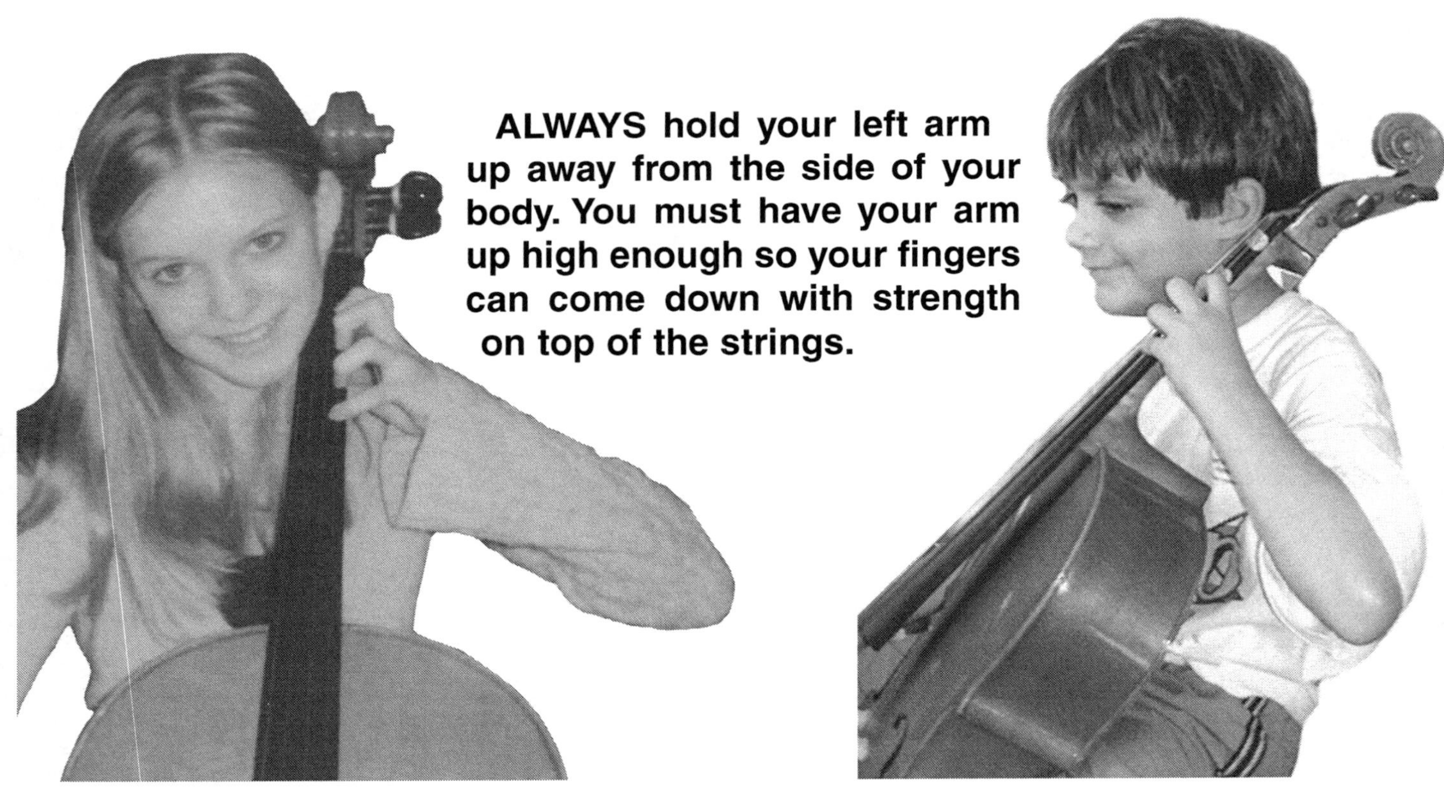

ALWAYS hold your left arm up away from the side of your body. You must have your arm up high enough so your fingers can come down with strength on top of the strings.

USING YOUR LEFT HAND

ARCH YOUR WHOLE HAND
INCLUDING YOUR THUMB.
Shape your hand as if you
were going to catch a ball.
Your fingers and you're thumb
should make a strong C shape.

FROM YOUR KNUCKLES TO YOUR
ELBOW SHOULD BE A STRAIGHT
LINE. Also, ALWAYS keep your hand
and arm up high so your fingers can
come down hard on top of the strings.

Your LEFT ARM should be about 10 inches from the side of your body.
Each finger needs to stand alone and move independently.
Each finger must also work as a team with the others.
Each finger must also calculate it's moves in relation
to what is coming next in the music.

Play every finger on every string slowly.

A STRING:	**0**	**1**	**2**	**3**	**4**	**4**	**3**	**2**	**1**	**0**
D STRING:	**0**	**1**	**2**	**3**	**4**	**4**	**3**	**2**	**1**	**0**
G STRING:	**0**	**1**	**2**	**3**	**4**	**4**	**3**	**2**	**1**	**0**
C STRING:	**0**	**1**	**2**	**3**	**4**	**4**	**3**	**2**	**1**	**0**

A STRING
IS
THE TOP LINE

A	B	C	C♯	D
0	1	2	3	4

SAY AND PLAY

First space on top of the staff B.

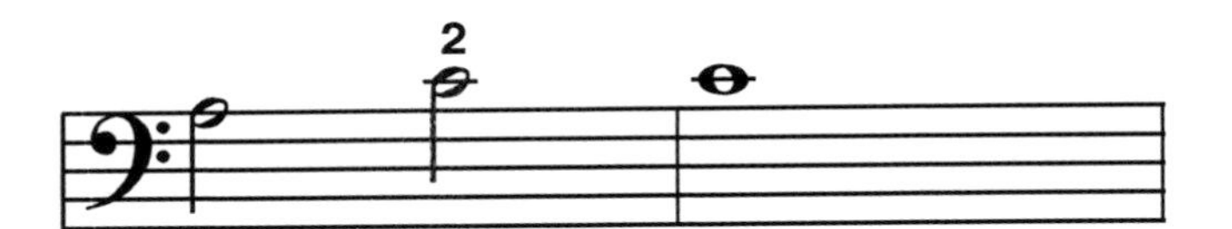

First line on top of the staff C.

First line on top of staff C♯.

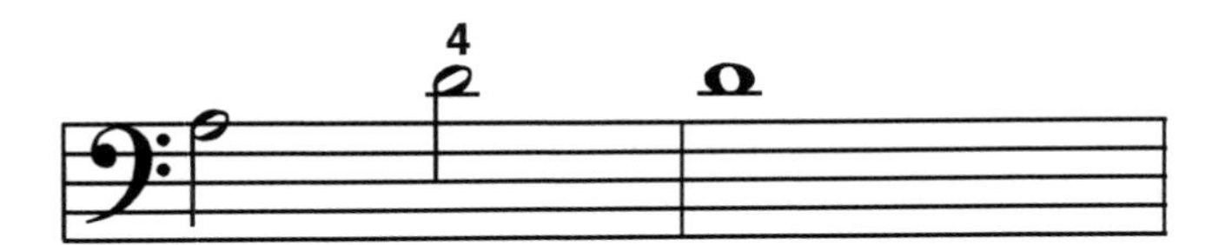

Second space on top of the staff D.

WRITE THE NOTES

B is 1

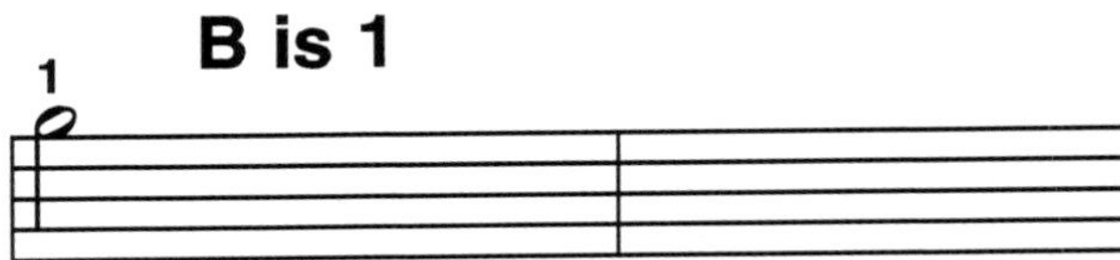

Play B with first finger.

C is 2

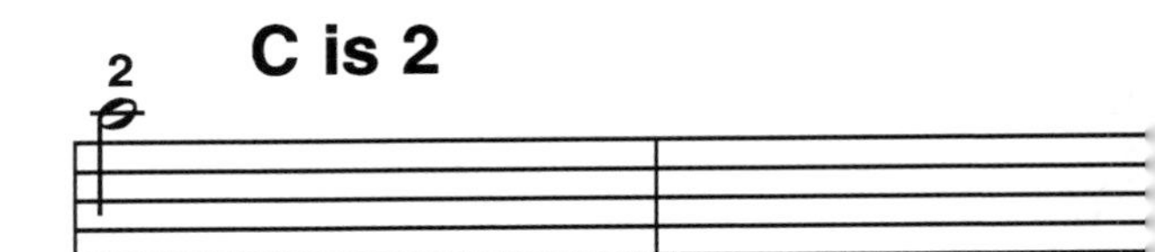

Play C with second finger.

C♯ is 3

Play C♯ with third finger.

D is 4

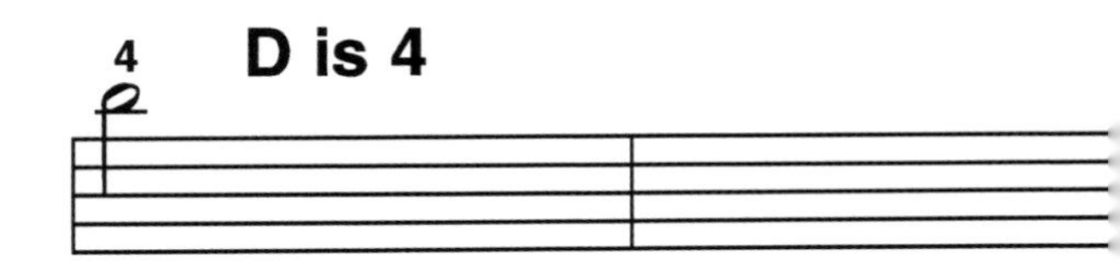

Play D with fourth finger.

ALL IN A ROW

Say each note before you play it.

A STRING
What note?
What finger?
What string?
Each finger plays one note higher, which is also the next letter in the alphabet.
A 0
B 1
C 2
C♯ 3
D 4
A B C C♯ D
1 2 3 4
D C♯ C B A
4 3 2 1 0
0 1 1 2 3 4 4 0 4 3 4
CLAIRE DE LA LUNE
0 0 0 1 3 1 0 3 1 1 0

D STRING
IS
THE MIDDLE LINE

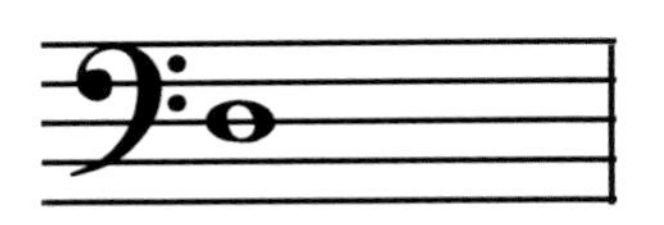

D	E	F	F♯	G
0	1	2	3	4

Take as much time as you need, memorize where each note is.

SAY AND PLAY

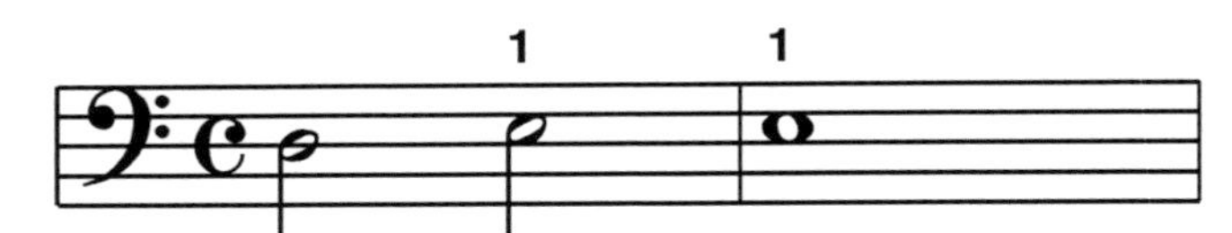

Third space from the bottom is E.

Fourth line from the bottom is F.

Fourth line from the bottom is F♯.

Top space is G.

WRITE THE NOTES

E is 1

1

Play E with first finger.

F is 2

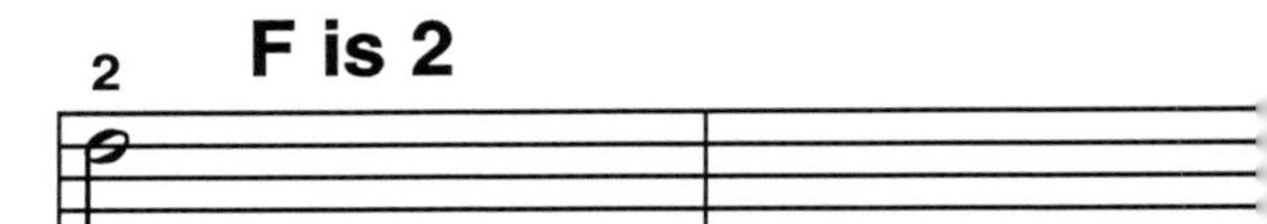

Play F with second finger.

F♯ is 3

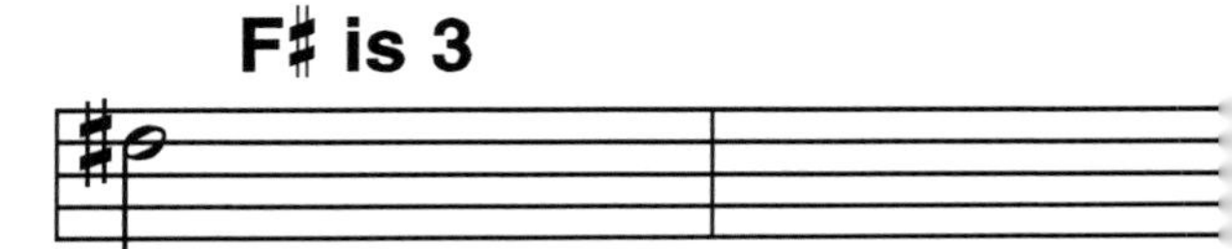

Play F♯ with third finger.

G is 4

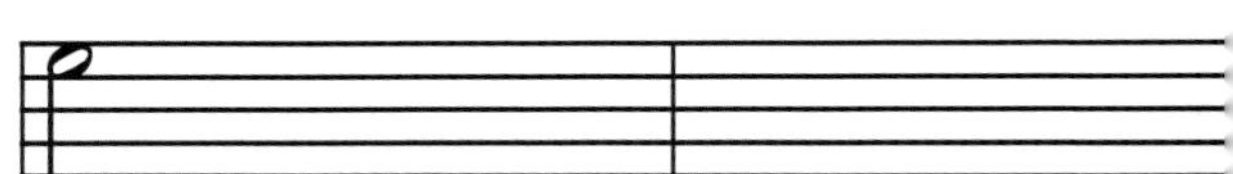

Play G with fourth finger.

ALL IN A ROW

Say each note before you play it.

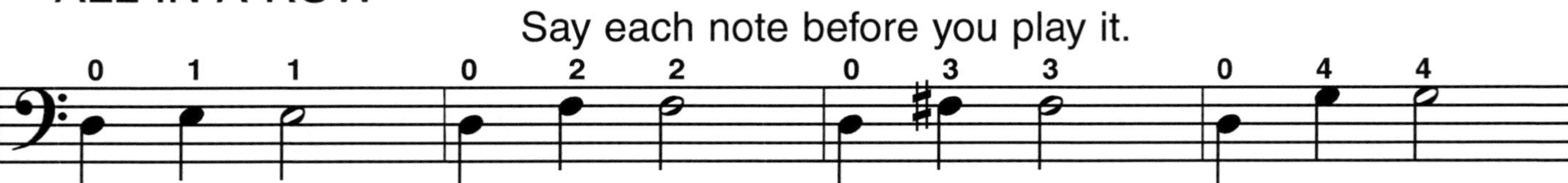

D STRING

What finger?
What note?
What string?

To read music you must be able to describe in words where each note is.

G STRING
IS
THE BOTTOM LINE

G	A	B♭	B	C
0	1	2	3	4

SAY AND PLAY

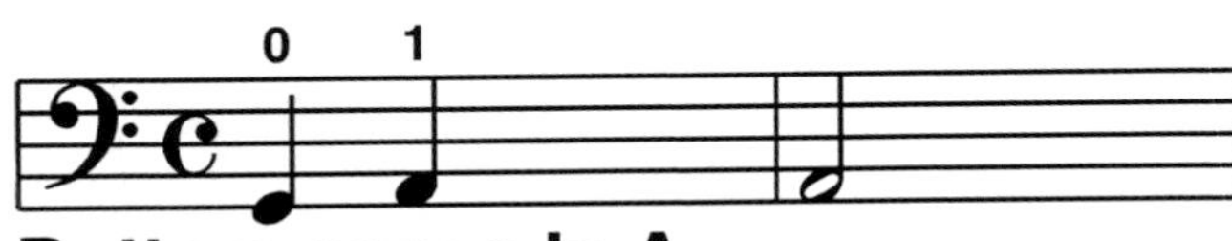

Bottom space is A.

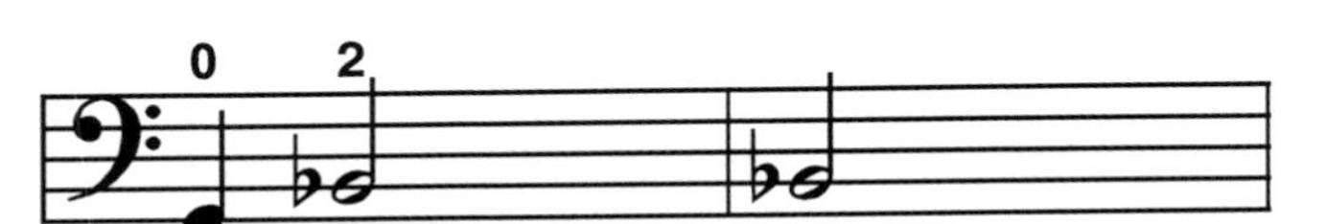

First line up from the bottom is B♭.

First line up from the bottom is B.

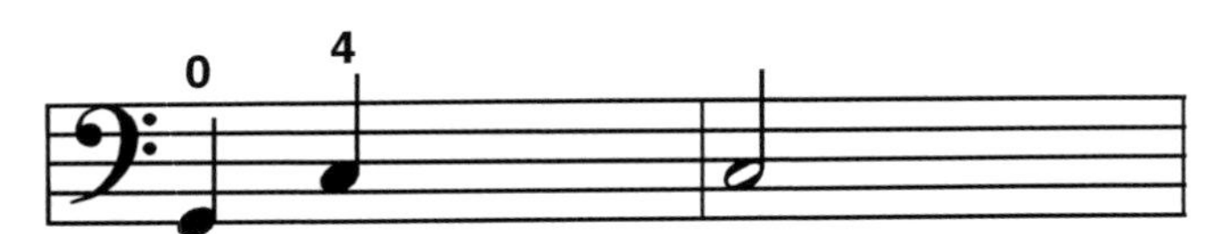

Second space up from the bottom is C.

WRITE THE NOTES

A is 1

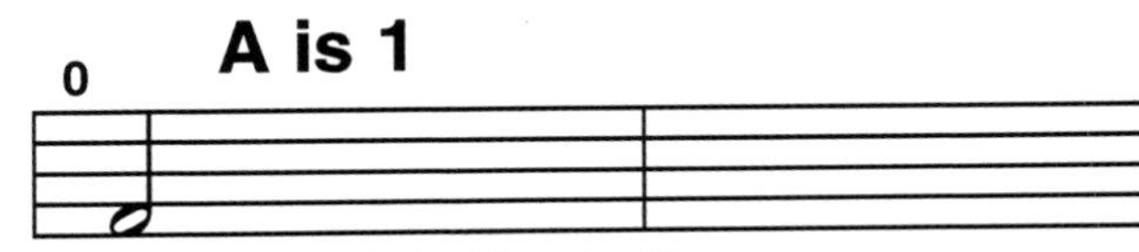

Play A with first finger.

B♭ is 2

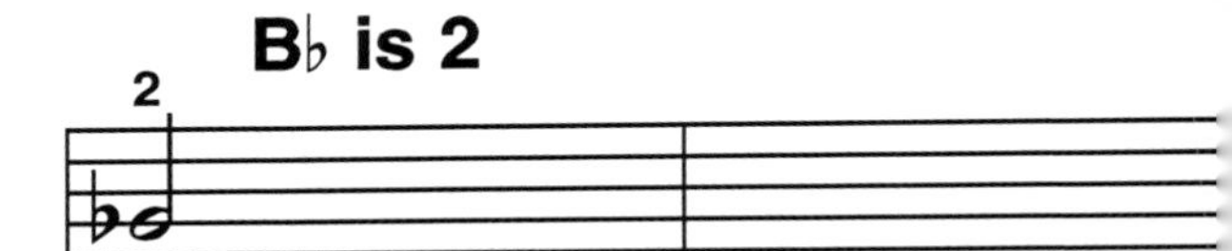

Play B♭ with second finger.

B is 3

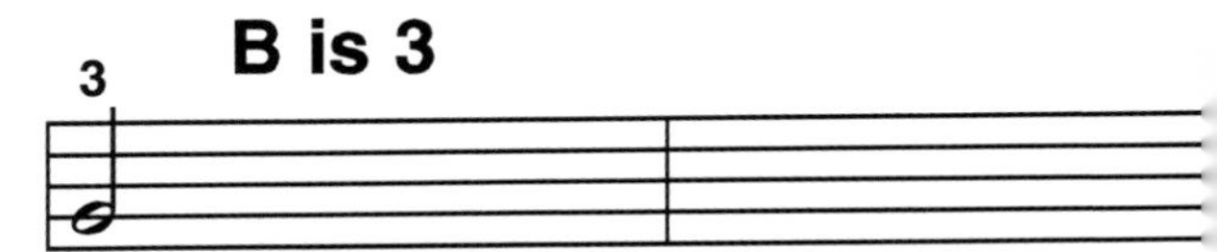

Play B with third finger.

C is 4

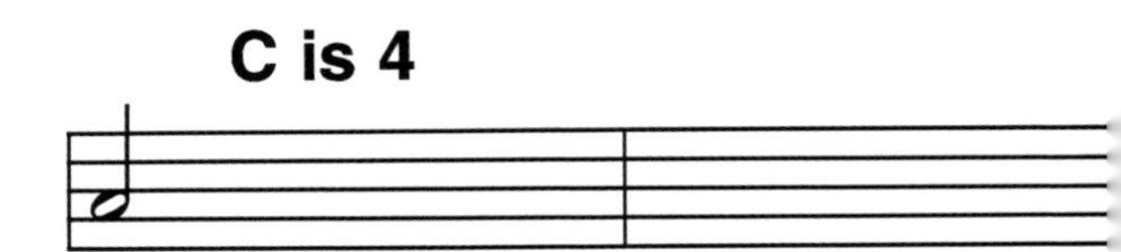

Play C with fourth finger.

ALL IN A ROW

G STRING

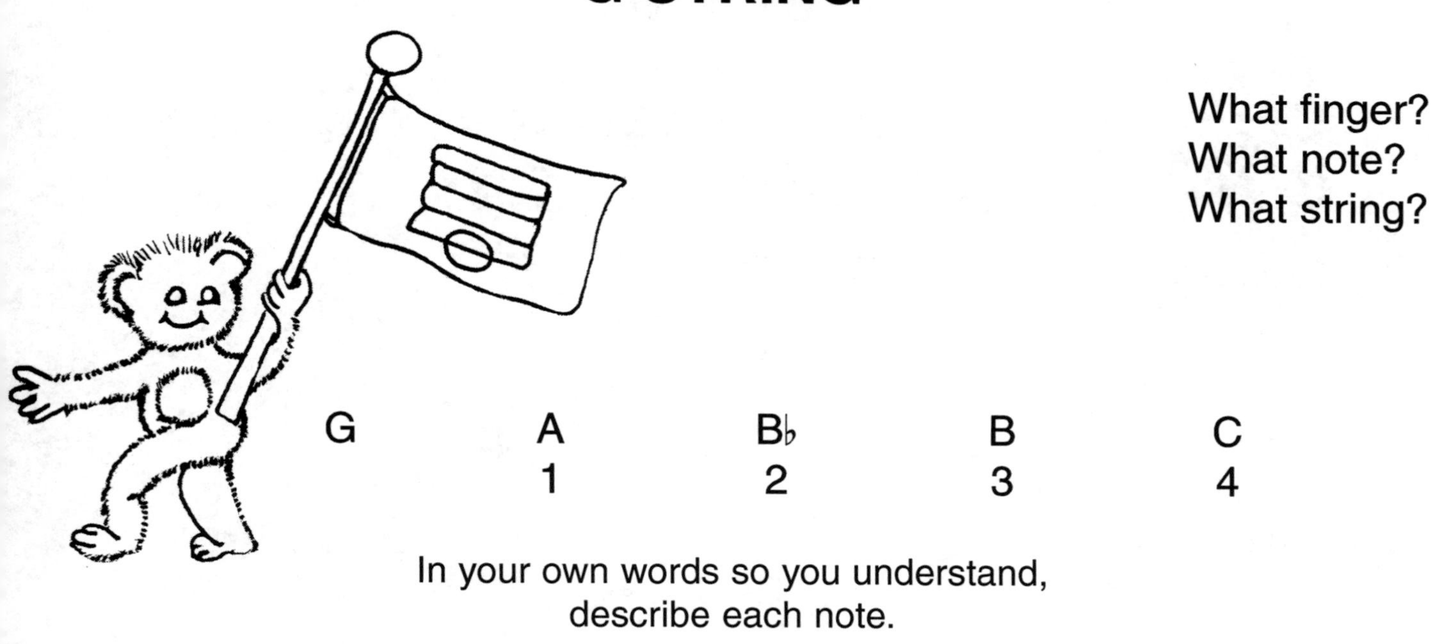

What finger?
What note?
What string?

G	A	B♭	B	C
	1	2	3	4

In your own words so you understand,
describe each note.

HOT CROSS BUNS

C STRING
IS
TWO LINES BELOW

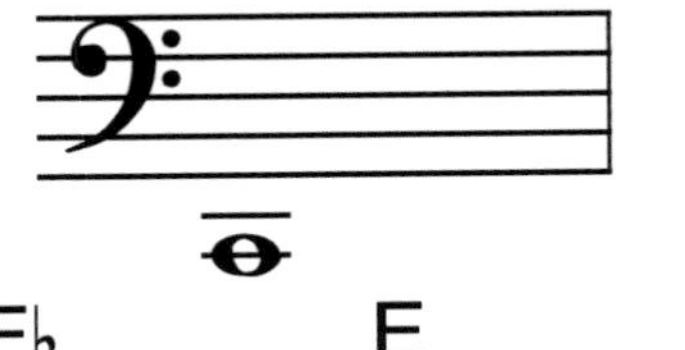

C	D	E♭	E	F
0	1	2	3	4

SAY AND PLAY

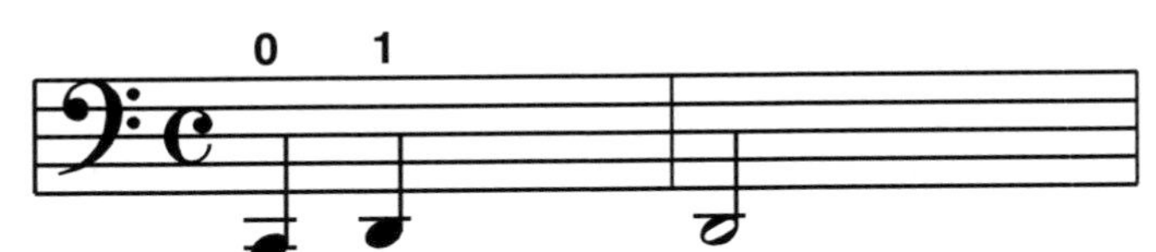

Two spaces below the staff is D.

One line below the staff is E♭.

One line below the staff is E.

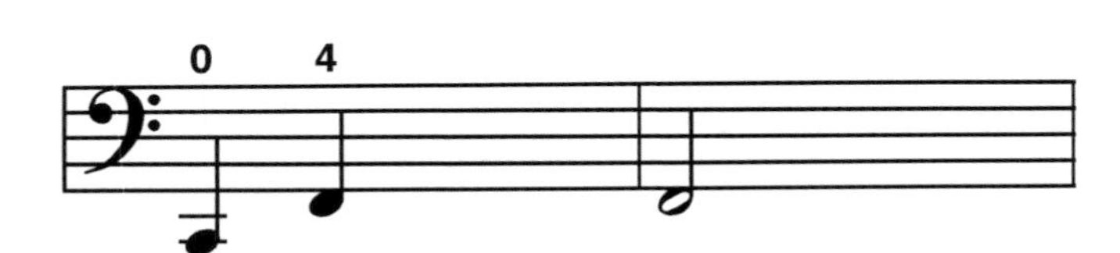

First space below the staff is F.

WRITE THE NOTES

D is 1

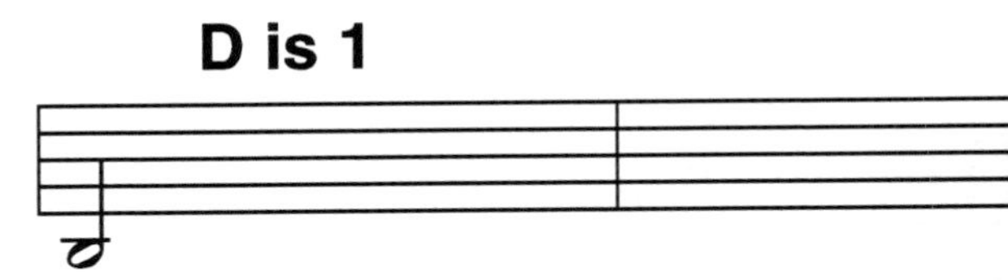

Play D with first finger.

E♭ is 2

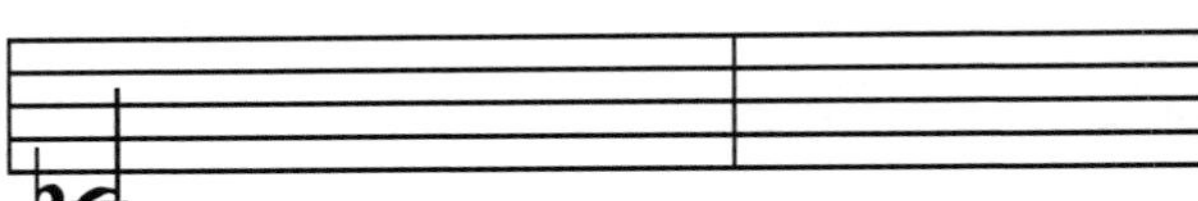

Play E♭ with second finger.

E is 3

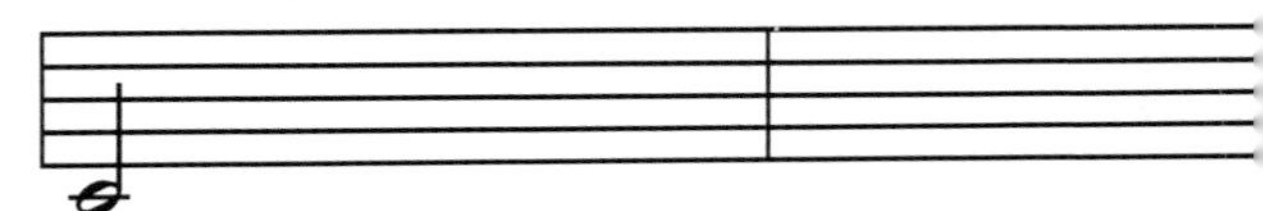

Play E with third finger.

E♭ is 4

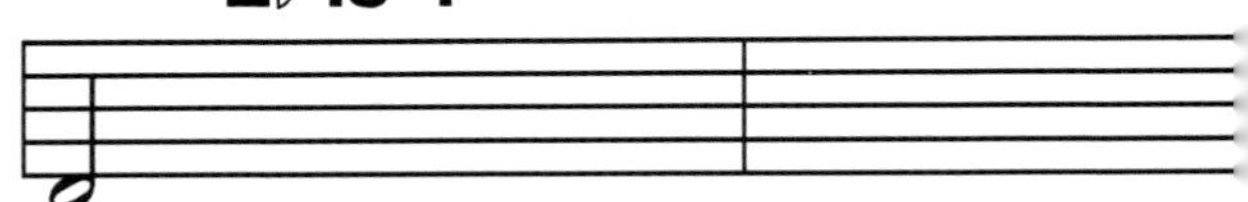

Play F with fourth finger.

ALL IN A ROW

C STRING

What finger?
What note?
What string?

Start with your 1st finger and you will see that each finger plays one note higher.

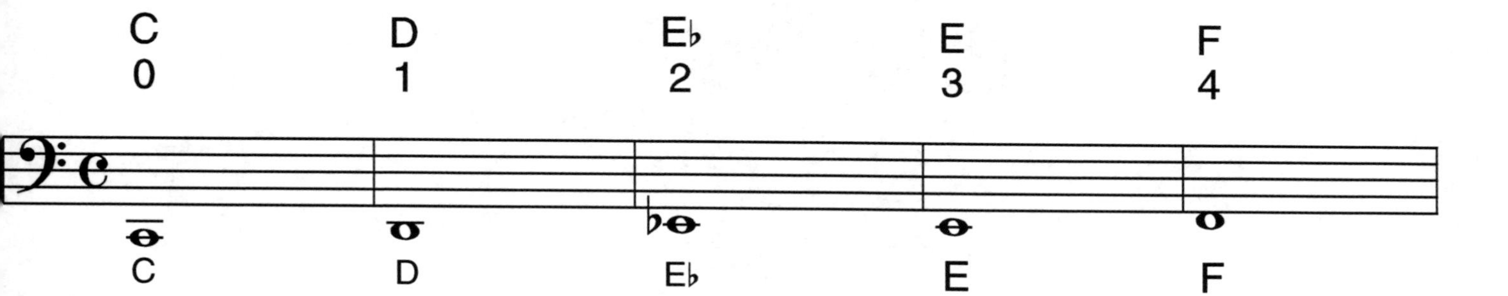

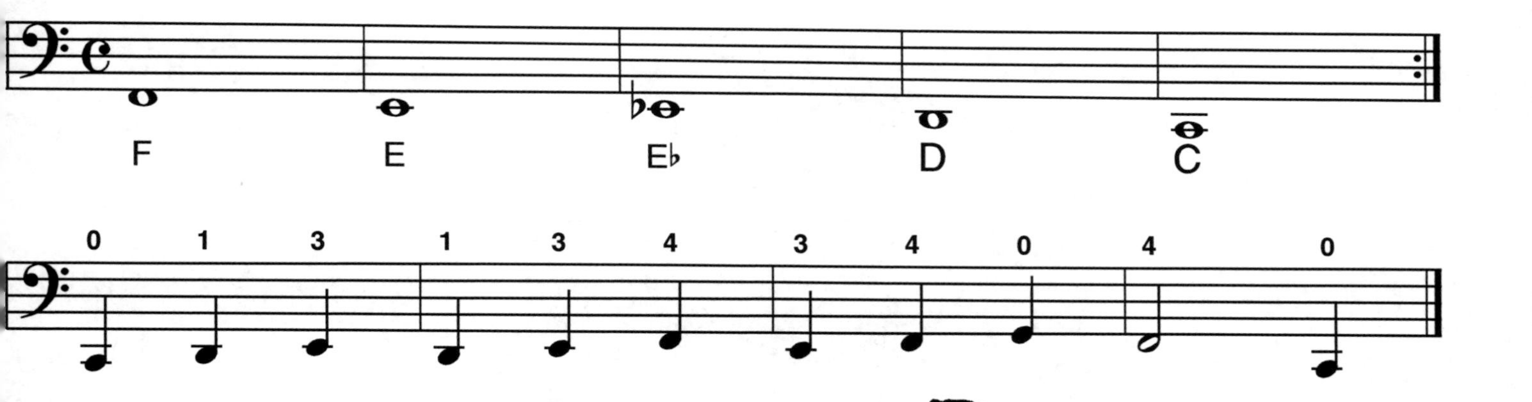

PONY RIDE

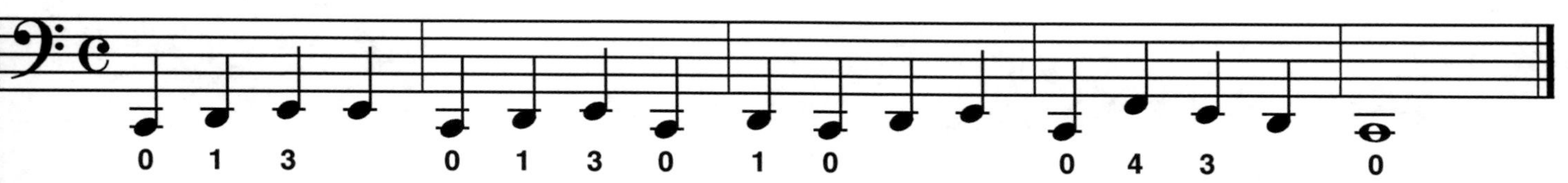

SONGS EVERYONE LOVES
BOWING EXERCISES
FINGER EXERCISES
THE SLUR
DOTTED NOTES

FOCUS: Make your notes sound clear and
pretty like the midnight sky.

TWINKLE TWINKLE LITTLE STAR

To make playing Twinkle Twinkle easier,
practice this exercise carefully.

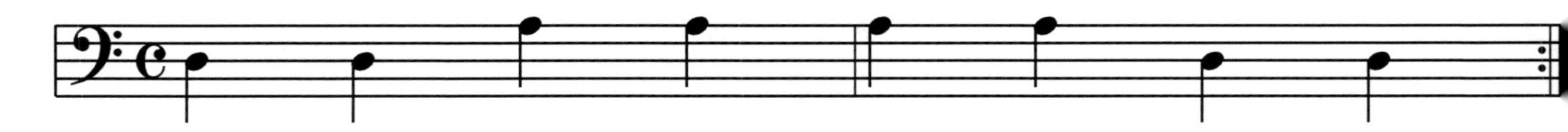

If you put a dot after a note; it means you are supposed to add ½ the value of the note onto it's original value.
A DOTTED ½ NOTE = 3 BEATS

𝅗𝅥 = 2 BEATS

• = ADD 1 BEAT
2 plus 1 = 3 beats

FRENCH SONG

NEW SKILL: Learning to practice.
To make learning easier, take a few notes from a song by themselves, and play them over and over until you know which finger goes where when. Then the song will make sense.

OLD MAC DONALD
Old Mac Donald had a farm, ee i ee i o And on this farm he had a cow
ee i ee i o With a moo moo here and a moo moo there Here a moo there a moo every where a
moo moo.... Old Mac Donald had a farm ee i ee i o.

ELEPHANTS
FOCUS:
Use your bow to make your notes sound like giant heavy feet.
I love el - e - phants, I love big gray el - e - phants.
MUD SONG
C♯ is third finger.
Mud, mud, glo - ri - ous mud,
Noth - ing quite like it for cool - ing your blood.
Fol - low me, fol - low, Down to the hol - low,
Where we will wal - low in glo - ri - ous mud.

FINGER EXERCISES

Before you start, to make playing easier put all your fingers in place. This includes your thumb which goes under your second finger.

Three things for you to do.

BUILD STRENGTH:
Bang your fingers down.

BECOME ACCURATE:
Exactly where is each note?

GAIN SPEED:
Repetition, play over and over.

RULES FOR FINGER EXERCISES

With your left hand make a shape as if you were about to catch a baseball. Now take that strongly arched hand and put your fingers on the strings and your thumb underneath.

RAISE YOUR LEFT ARM UP AND KEEP IT AWAY FROM THE SIDE OF YOUR BODY. Your arm should be at least 10 inches from the side of your body.

Start with ALL FOUR FINGERS OVER THE STRINGS and leave them there. All four fingers should be ready in case you need them in a hurry.

Keep your whole hand arched, including your thumb. Try very hard to bend your thumb out also. Keep your thumb under your 2nd finger.

FOCUS: Make your first and fourth fingers stay far enough apart so they are both in tune at the same time.
You have to spread your fingers slightly. Check your fourth finger with the string below to see if they are the same.

EXERCISE FOR BOW CONTROL AND CELLO SOUND

Here's how to learn the most with this bowing exercise.

1. Play 4 short bows at the frog using mostly your wrist to make the bow move.
2. Play one long bow all the way to the tip with a big clear sound. Watch your bow and bow arm.
3. Play 4 short bows way out at the tip. Watch and listen carefully to make a clear sound.
4. Play one long bow all the way back down to the frog and repeat the whole series.

Move your bow with your wrist and your arm on the short notes, but keep a solid bow grip and stay in control.

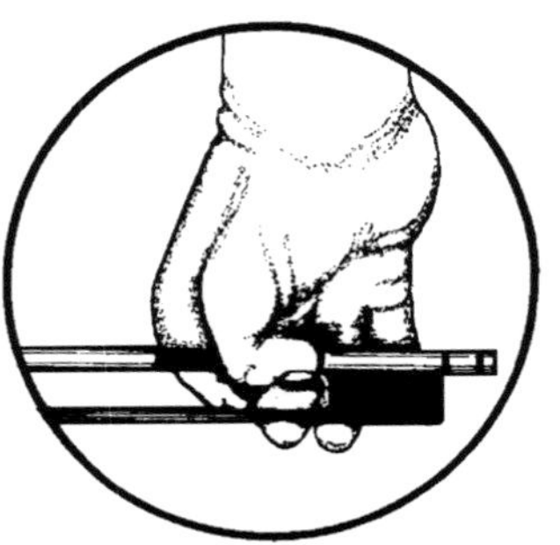

Also practice with your 2 middle fingers off the bow to strengthen your bow grip and 4th finger.

The more you watch your bow arm and pay close attention to what it is doing the better your notes will sound.

A short note uses less than 6 inches of bow.

BIRDS IN A TREE LOOKING DOWN AT ME

TWO BOWING EXERCISES

To help you learn bow control; practice all bowing exercises at least part of the time with your two middle fingers off your bow. This will also help you learn to use your fourth finger for control.

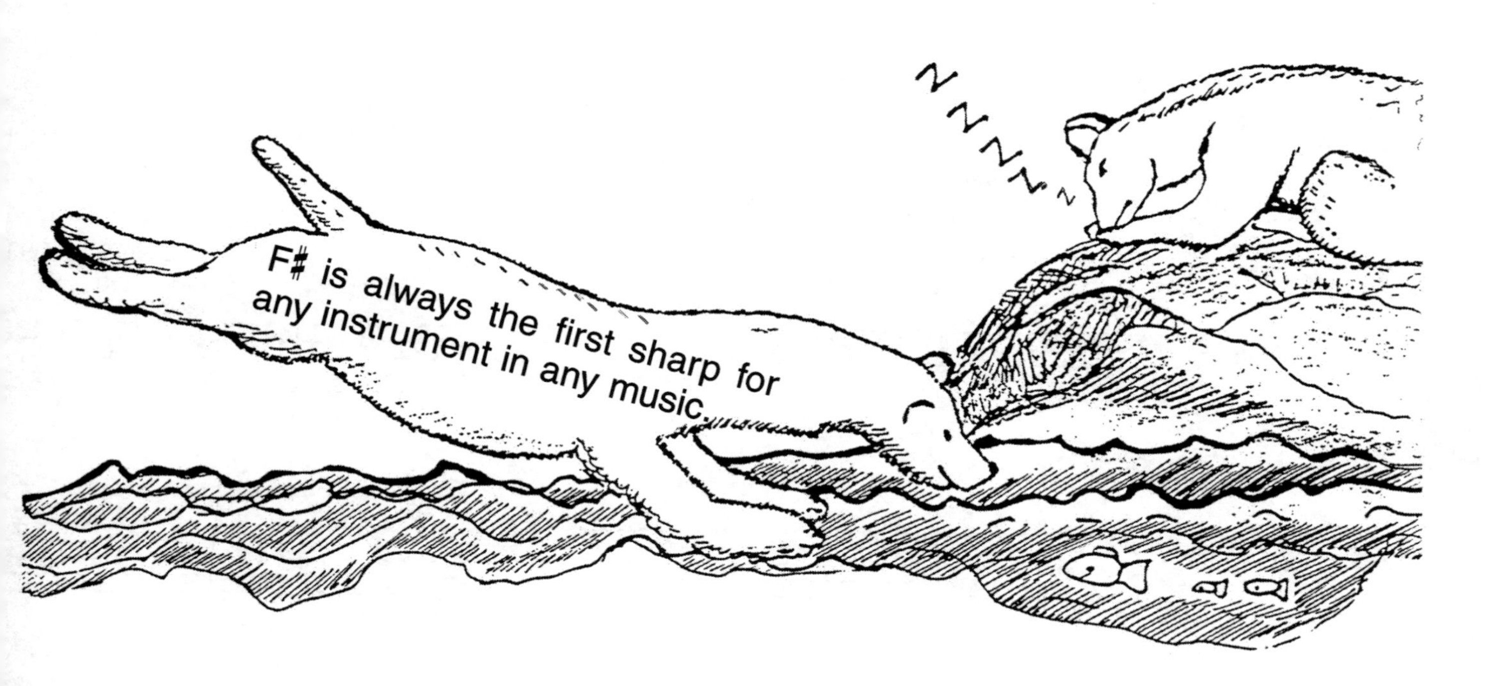

POLAR BEARS

Long smooth bows

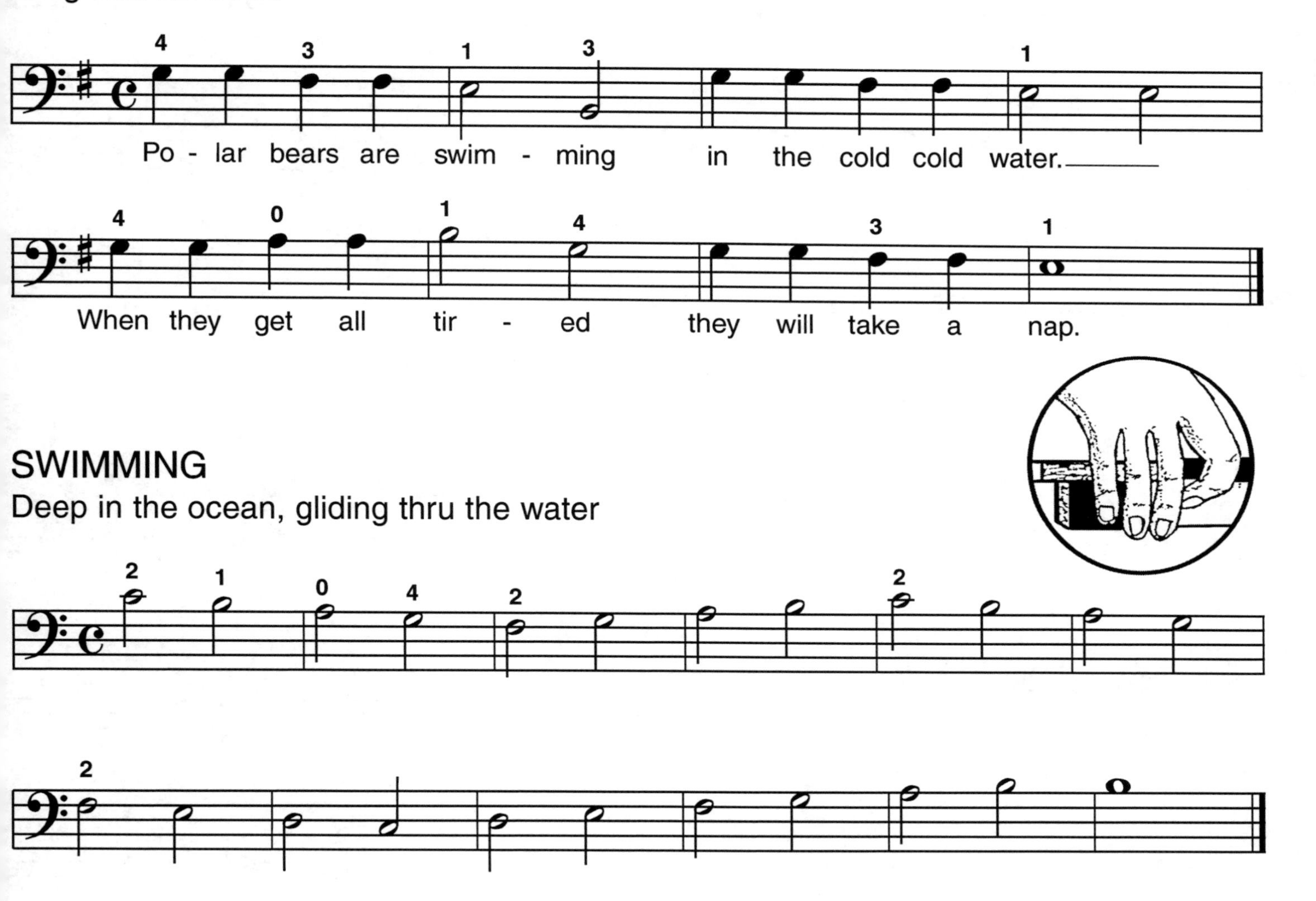

SWIMMING

Deep in the ocean, gliding thru the water

ODE TO JOY

FOCUS: Play with big beautiful bow strokes, as if you are the chorus and orchestra all in one.

Beethoven

PACHELBEL CANON

FOCUS: Use very long bows on the half notes and make the cello ring like a bell.

Pachelbel

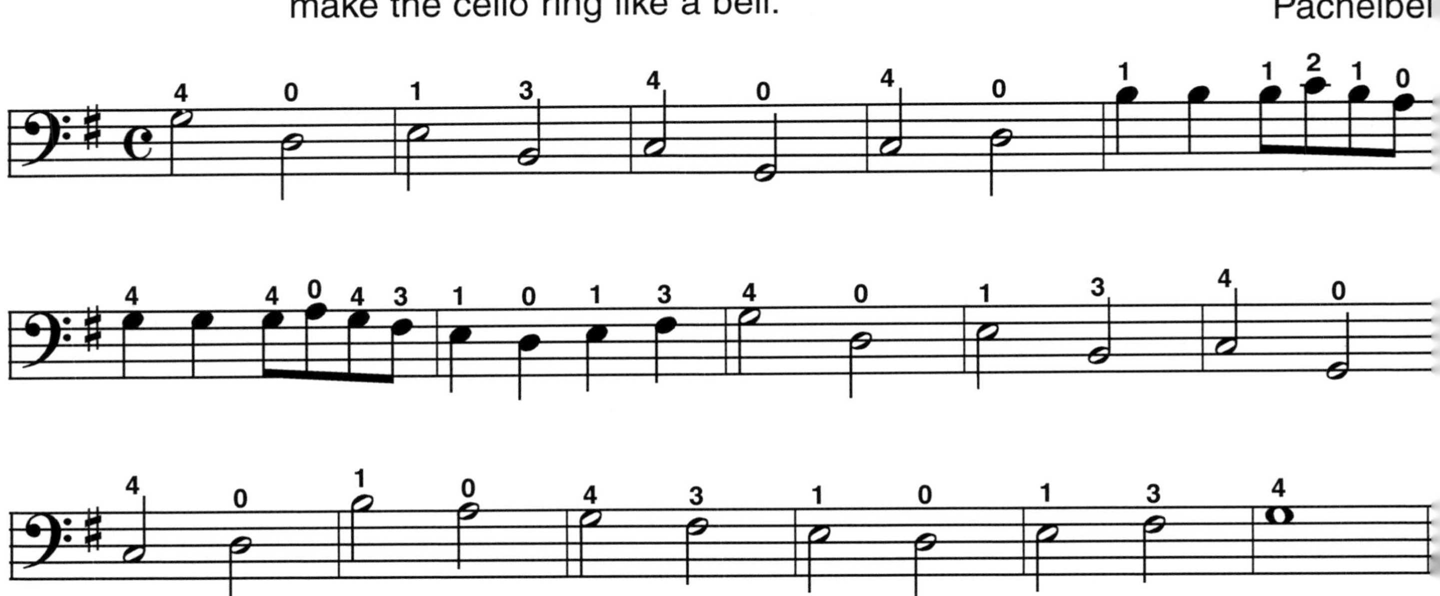

ONE NOTE AT THE BEGINNING OF A PIECE IS CALLED A PICK UP.
A PICK UP IS ALMOST ALWAYS UP BOW.

COUNTRY DANCE

Beethoven

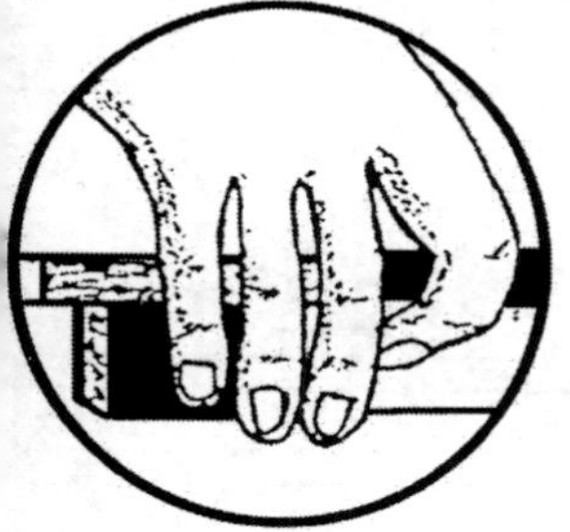

Use a long slow bow on the half note. Move your bow faster on the quarter note to get back to the frog in time.

Count carefully. Two beats on the half note, one beat only on the quarter note.

HUMPTY DUMPTY

THE SLUR

A slur is more than one note in a bow.
A slur will produce a smooth even sound.

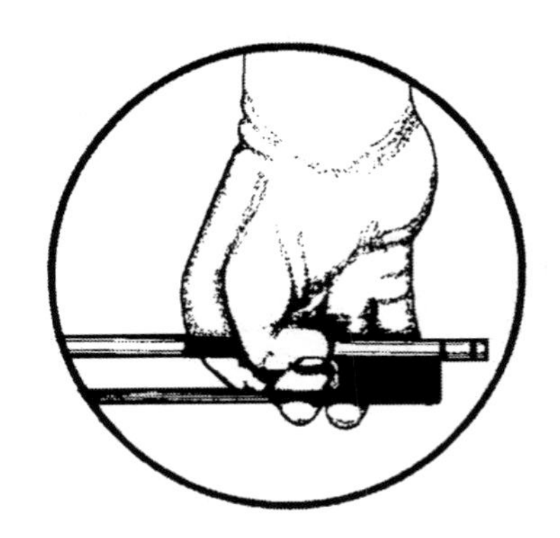

Use your whole bow.

Each note needs ½ of your bow.
Make sure both notes sound good.

Use a smooth motion to cross the string and move just far enough up or down to hit only one string at a time.
No extra noises please.

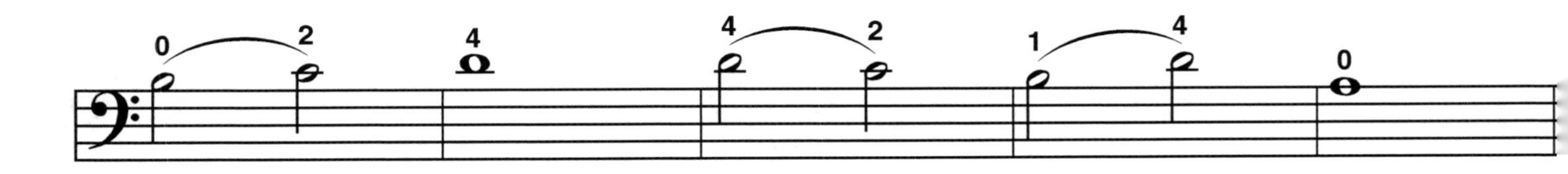

FOCUS: Use your whole bow.
Each note needs ½ your bow.

Use a smooth motion to cross the strings and move just far enough up or down to hit only one string at a time.

Make sure you use your whole bow on the down bow
So you will have enough space for the up bow.

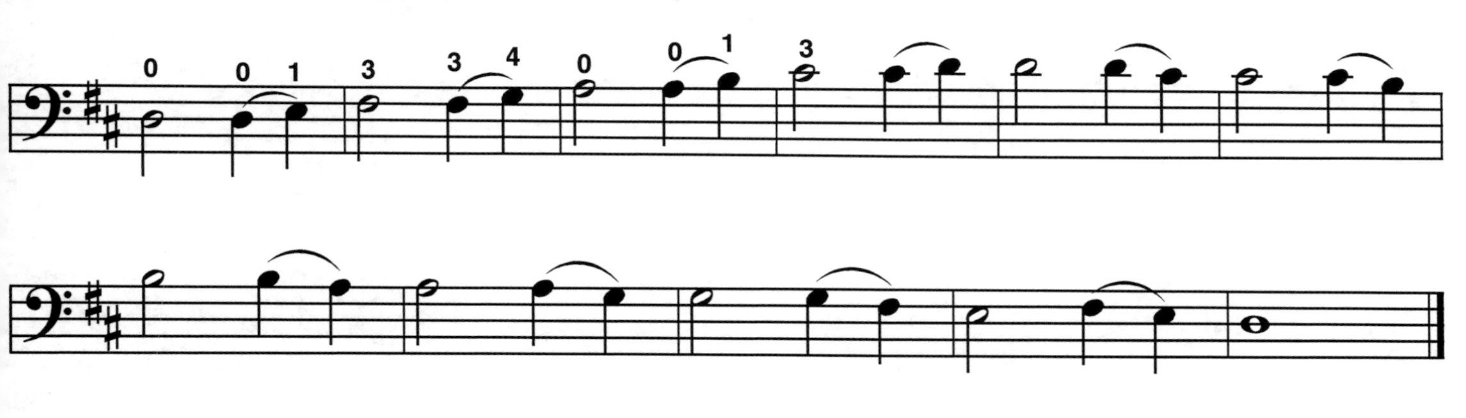

LONG LONG AGO

T. Bayly

Reminder: F♯ = 3rd finger F♮ = 2nd finger

NOW WE WILL DANCE

Use short bows on the eighth notes and long ones on the quarter notes.

DANCERS IN THE SUN

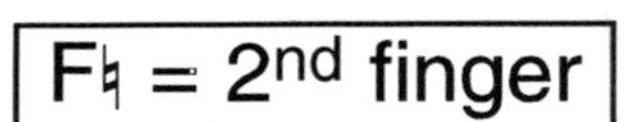

HAYDN'S SURPRISE
F♮ = 2nd finger
4 1 4 1 2
WALKING SONG
4 1 4 1
Let's go wal - king in the for - est. Let's go wal - king all day long.
RUNNING SONG
F♯ and
C♯ = 3rd
Finger
FOCUS: Place your fingers firmly but carefully on the notes.
Move with a clean sound from one note to the next.
Strong fingers make a beautiful sound.
0 1 3 4 3 4 0 1 0 1 3 4

I'M A LITTLE TEA POT
I'm a litt-le tea pot short and stout, here is my han-dle here is my spout.
When I'm hot and stea-my, hear me out. Tip me o - ver pour me out!

HOT CROSS BUNS
Hot cross buns, hot cross buns, one a pen-ny two a pen-ny
hot cross buns. If you have no daugh - ters, give them to your sons,
one a pen - ny two a pen - ny, hot cross buns!

SONG OF THE WIND

Make the wind blow with your bow. Try to decide for yourself what you should do with your bow to make the wind sing.

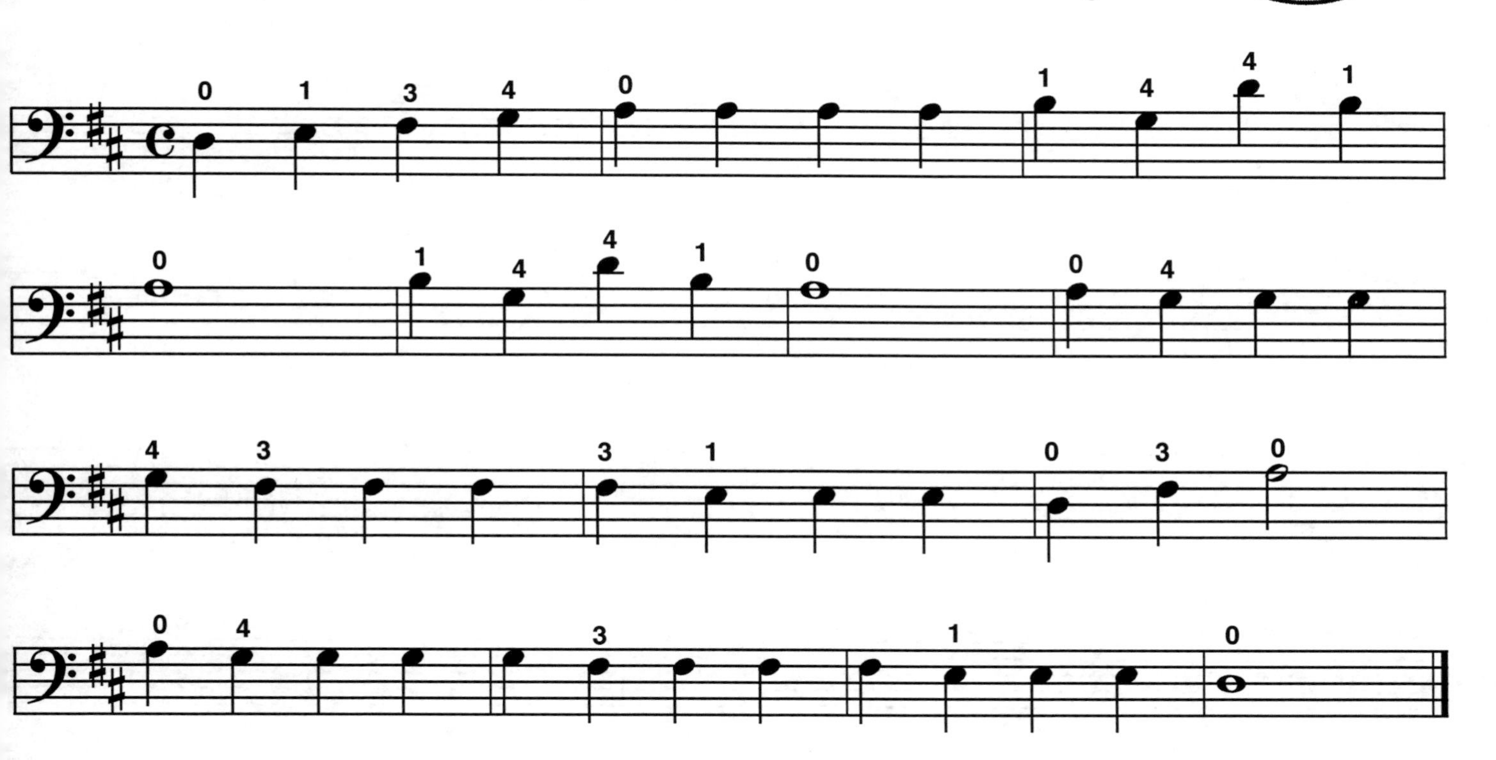

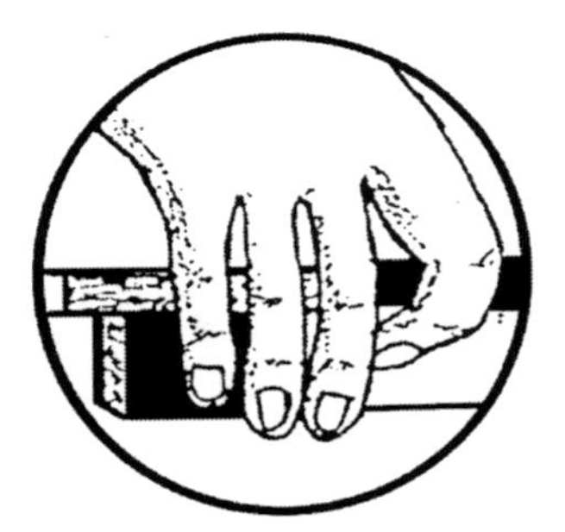

BEAN THE BASSET HOUND

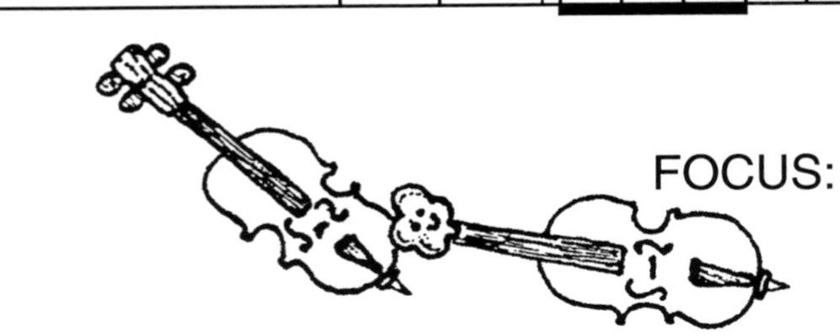

FOCUS: For both of these songs, make a big difference between the amount of bow you use for the quarter notes and the eighth notes.

WALTZ OF THE CELLOS

SING LITTLE ROBBIN
THE CUCKOO
FOCUS: Move your bow very fast on the one beat down bow so you'll have plenty of bow for the two beat up bow.
BRAHMS LULLABY
Play this gently, but with a clear sound so a baby could fall asleep while listening.

BOWING EXERCISE with variations

This is to help you learn to control your bow. You learn the easy notes and then you play them with the variations.

WB = Whole Bow

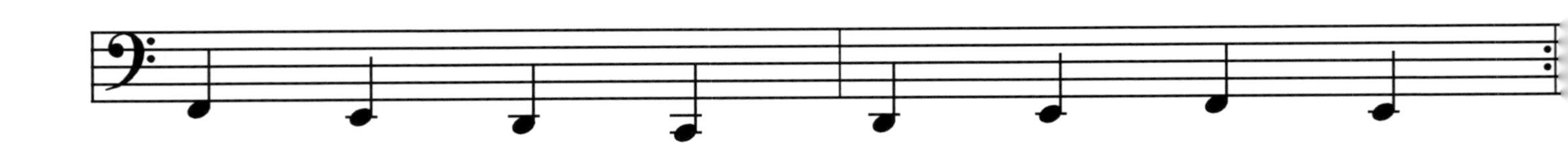

Use your whole bow. Go all the way from one end to the other on each note. Make a smooth change from down bow to up bow. Don' t stop, dig in or jerk your bow. Keep your bow moving smoothly as you change directions.

Play with all down bows creating a big circle with your arm as you lift your bow up after each note and bring it down to start the next note.

One long note with a whole bow; two shorter notes with one half bow each. Use twice as much bow on the longer notes as on the shorter ones.

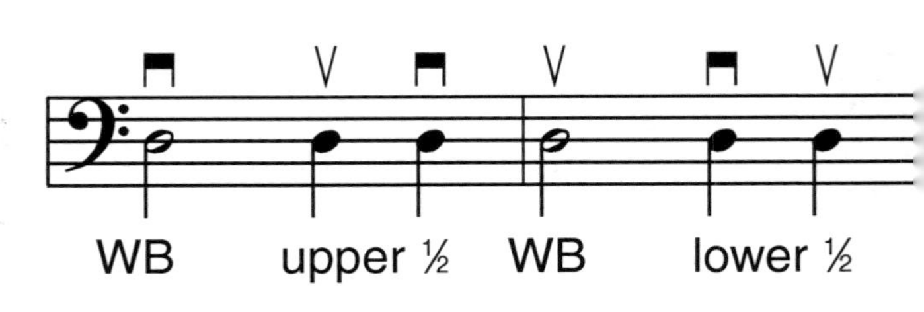

AS YOU PLAY, CONCENTRATE ON YOUR RIGHT ARM AND YOUR BOW. Try to perfect your bow grip and start learning how to control the motion of your bow. A steady hand, smooth motion from your arm, and a wrist that bends in on the up bow and out on the down bow is what you need.

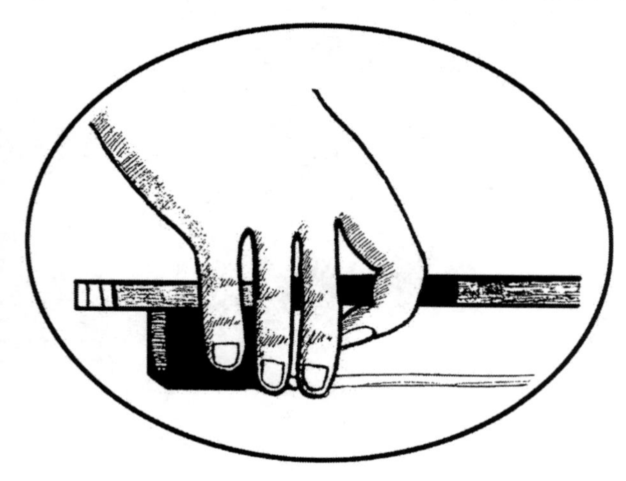

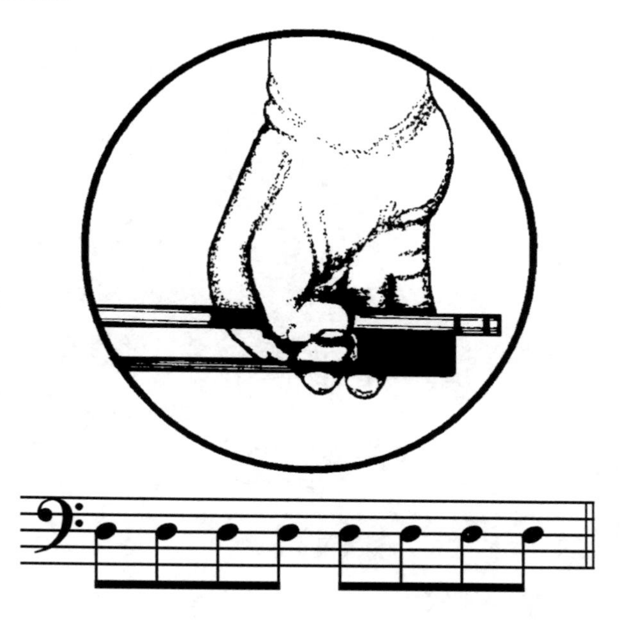

For these short notes use just a few inches of bow and keep your wrist bending in and out. Use your wrist to move the bow and move your arm as little as possible. Try the eighth notes at the frog and at the tip.

Use half of your bow for each note. Two quarter notes in a bow means use ½ your bow for each note.

Learn to judge how much bow you need for each note to fit them all in one slur and make them all sound good.

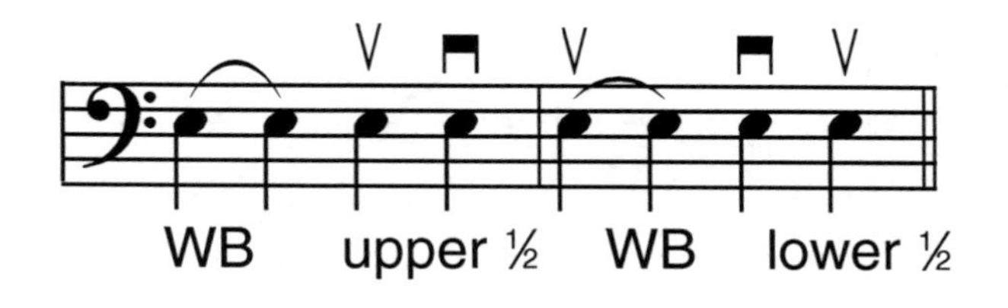

Now you play two slurred then two separate notes. First you play two notes in one long bow, then two short bows either way out at the tip or way down at the frog.

Play two slurred, using one ½ bow each.
Play two short bows each for two notes.
Play two slurred, using ½ bow each.
Play two short bows each for two notes.

FOR STRENGTH AND SPEED

ALWAYS keep your arm up away from the side of your body. NEVER bend your wrist. Make sure there is a straight line from your knuckles to your elbow!

MARCH IN D
Bach
0 1 3
DUET
Dotzaur
2

Don't forget to use
less bow on the 8th notes.
SIMPLE GIFTS
Shaker son
DUET
Mozar

2 = Two beats in a measure
4 = A quarter note gets one beat

Play with long smooth bows.
FOCUS:How should you divide
your bow so all three notes
fit in and sound good?
MORNING MOOD
Greig
Peaceful and dreamy......
COUNTRY FAIR DAY
Fun and energetic
Watts

HUSH LITTLE BABY

Play with smooth gentle bow strokes.
Make a soothing sound with your cello.

If that diamond ring turns brass,
Momma's gonna buy you a looking glass.
If that looking glass gets broke,
Momma's gonna buy you a billy goat.

If that billy goat won't pull,
Moma's gonna buy you a cart and bull.
If that cart and bull fall down
You'll still be the sweetest little babe in town.

DOTTED NOTES

A dot after a note • adds on ½ the value of the note.

For example, a 1 beat note would become a 1½ beat note and a 2 beat note would become a 3 beat note.

If you accent the 8th note slightly as you count 1, 2, 3, 4, it will help you get the feel of dotted quarter, eighth.

Also play ♩. ♪ with a slur.

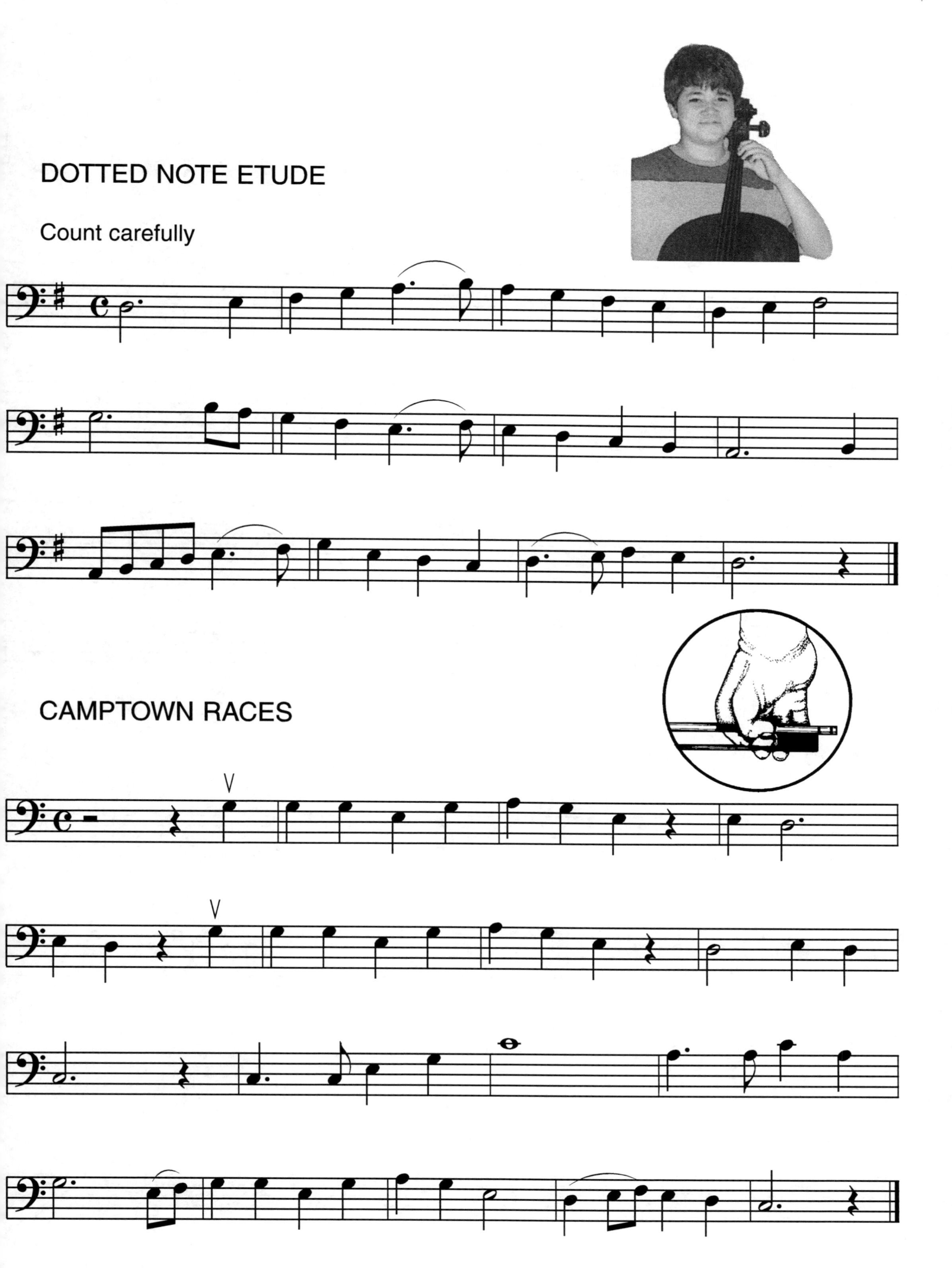
DOTTED NOTE ETUDE
Count carefully
CAMPTOWN RACES

OH COME LITTLE CHILDREN

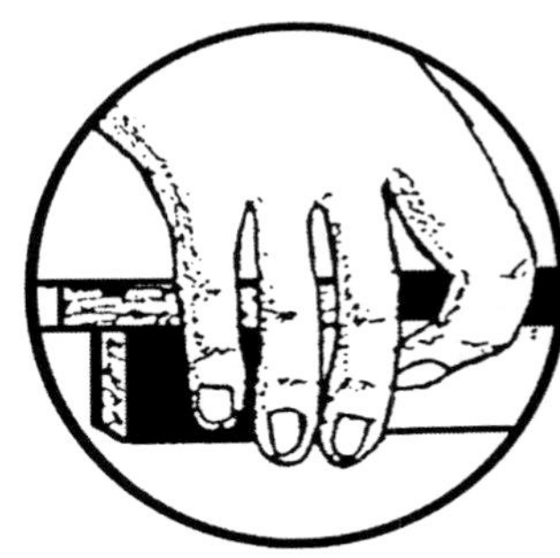

Always try to make your left hand round and strong.
Challenge: Can you keep your fingers pressed down on the D string while you play the open A string?

SHE'LL BE COMING ROUND THE MOUNTAIN

SONG FOR LUCKY

V = Up bow.
Move your bow to the right.

OH SUSANNAH

BETWEEN THE OX & THE GREY DONKEY

MARCH IN G

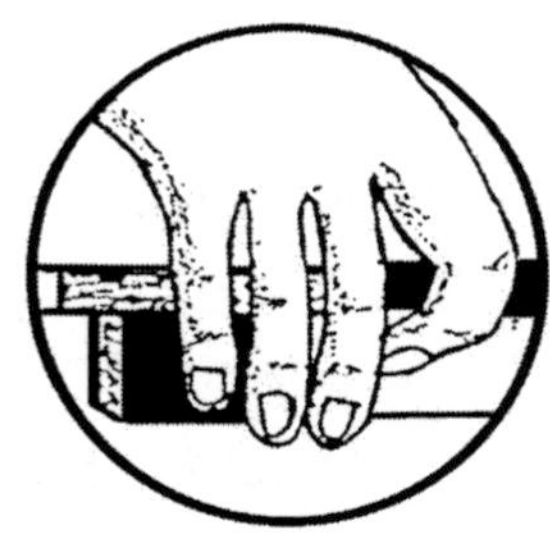

When you have two slurred notes that are the same pitch with either dots or lines over top, you make a graceful space between the two notes with your bow. You gently stop and then gracefully start up again going in the same direction.

TURKEY IN THE STRAW

Use very little bow on the eighth notes. The song goes quite fast, so you have to think ahead and stay in control.

ARKANSAS TRAVELER

MORE SONGS
DYNAMICS
BOWING
FINGER EXERCISES
ETUDES
DUETS

DYNAMICS

Make a piece of music interesting.

p = *piano* Play very softly

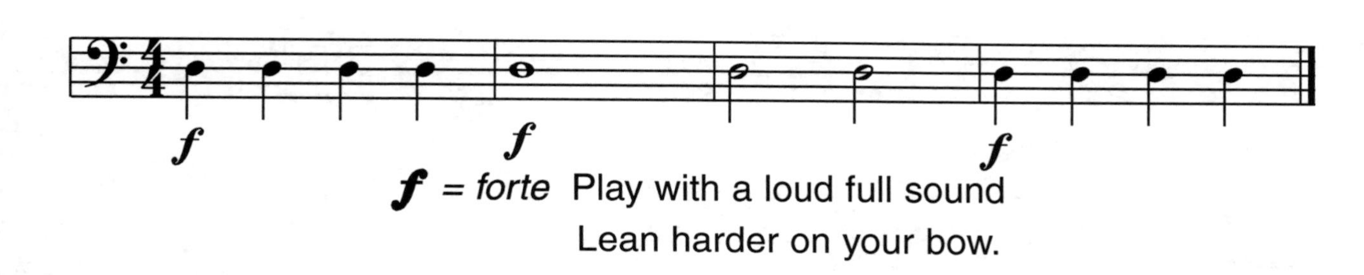

f = *forte* Play with a loud full sound
Lean harder on your bow.

Crescendo = get louder
It is written as cresc. in music.

Diminuendo = get softer.

= TRIPLETS, 3 NOTES TO A BEAT

USING THE RIGHT AMOUNT OF PRESSURE

If you press too hard, you will make an ugly choking sound. If you don't press enough, you will make a fuzzy sound.

Just like in Goldie Locks with the bear's beds, not too hard, not too soft, just right. You must figure out what is the right amount of pressure to make a beautiful sound.

It is also extremely important HOW MUCH bow you use and HOW FAST you move your bow.

STUDY IN TRIPLETS

Werner

MARCH OF THE TOY SOLDIERS

(from The Nutcracker)

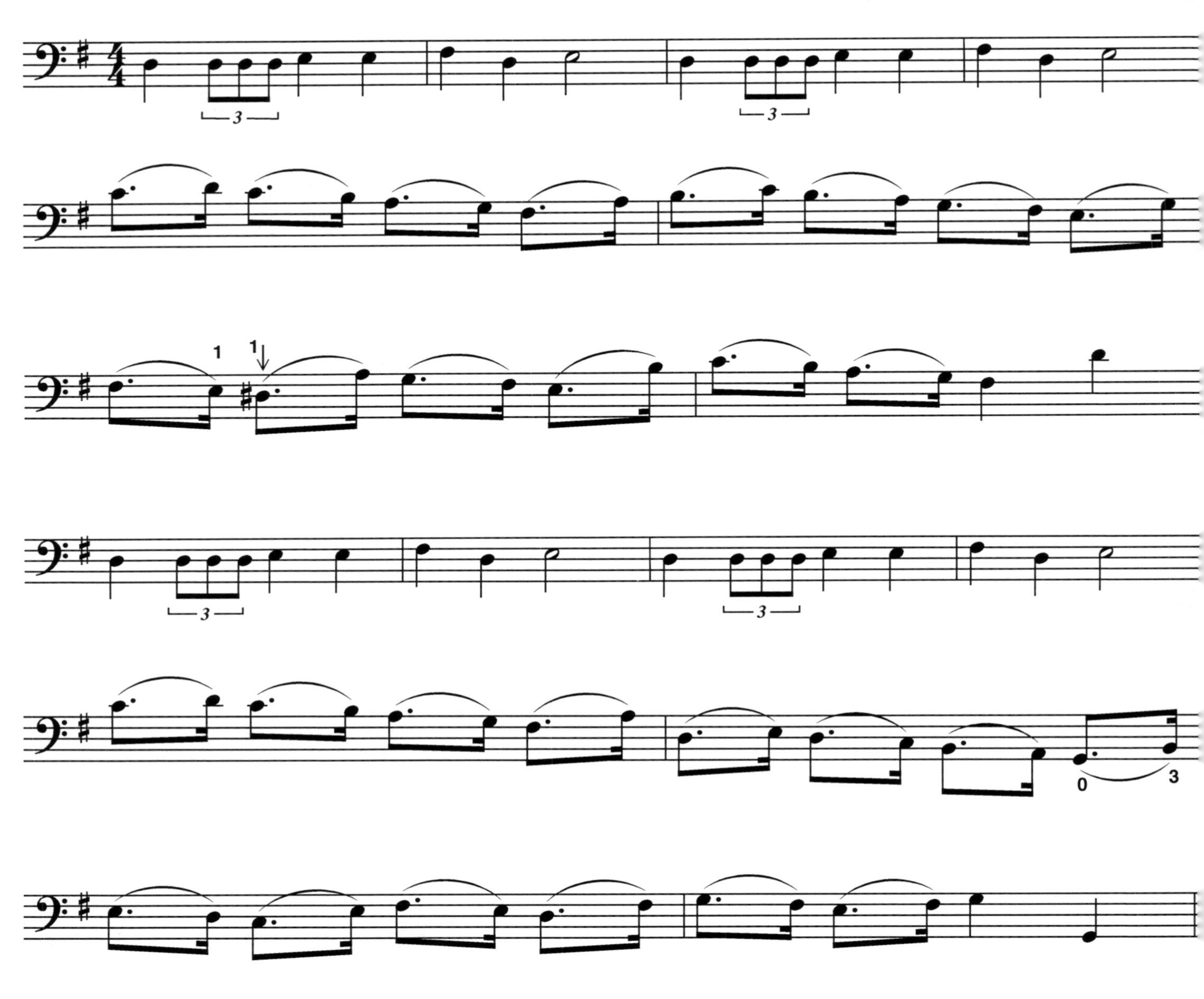

SOLDIER'S MARCH

Here's a chance for some bow fun! Make a big circle with your arm after each note to land down bow on the next note with a terrific sound.

THE LITTLE FIDDLE

Folk

REMEMBER
Dotted ¼ note gets 1½ beats.

EVENING PEACEFULLY SONG

Keep working to strengthen your left hand.
"Bang" your fingers down as you play each note.

MINUET IN C

Use lots of bow; make a big beautiful sound.

J. S. Bach

You need to be very sure of exactly how to hold your left hand and exactly what to do with each finger at all times to make clear, in tune, beautiful music.
That means you have to FOCUS completely on what your left hand is doing when you practice left-hand finger exercises. Play each line on all strings.

1. Arch your fingers.
2. Thumb under 2nd finger.
3. "Bang" your fingers down on each note.

Make sure you repeat each line.

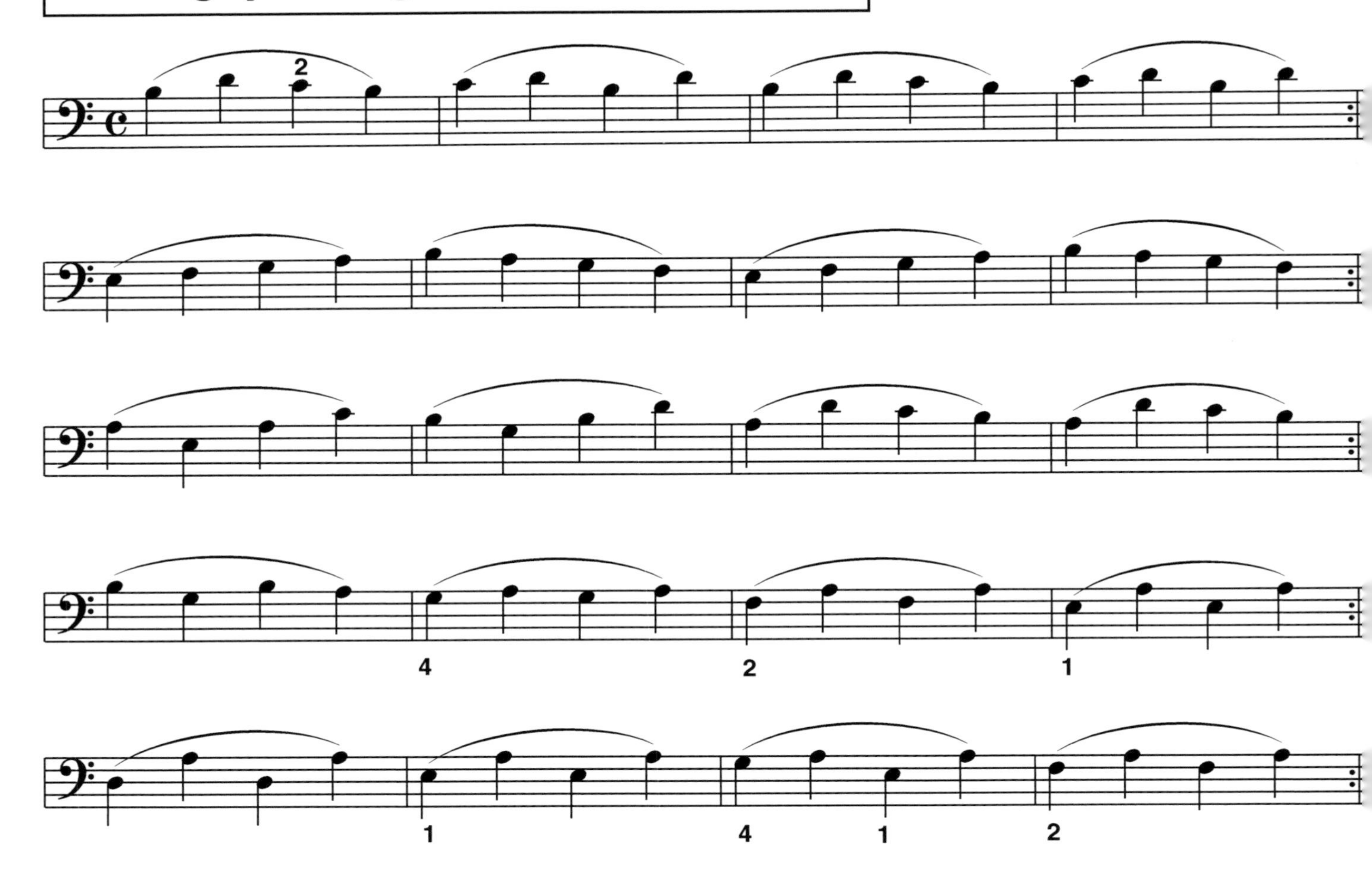

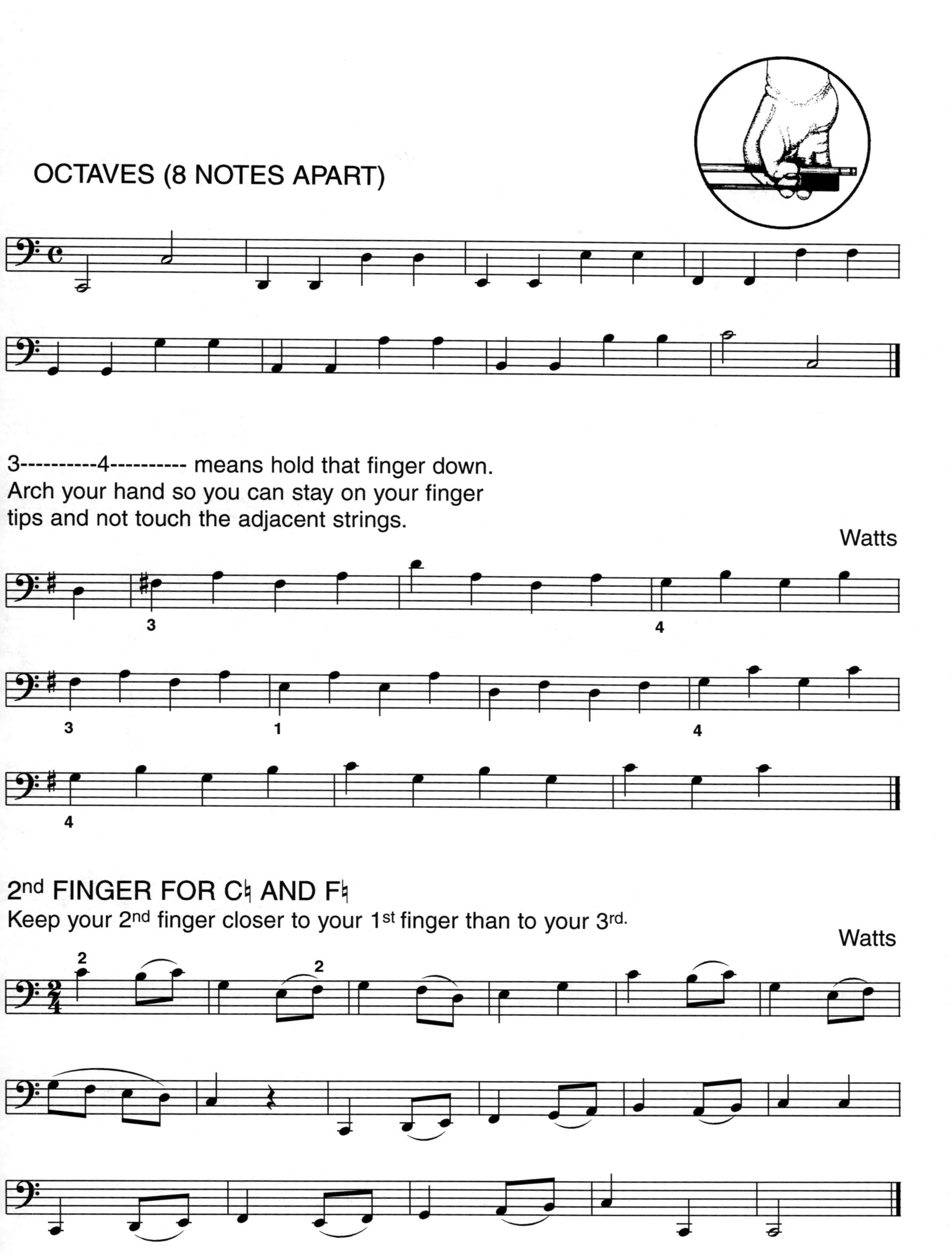
OCTAVES (8 NOTES APART)
3----------4---------- means hold that finger down.
Arch your hand so you can stay on your finger
tips and not touch the adjacent strings.
Watts
3
4
3
1
4
4
2nd FINGER FOR C♮ AND F♮
Keep your 2nd finger closer to your 1st finger than to your 3rd.
Watts
2
2

Keep all of your fingers over the strings at all times.
Look ahead and be prepared for the next note.
"Bang" your fingers down; work for strength.
Hold your two middle fingers off the bow.

Dotzaur

Arch your fingers round and strong.
Play on your fingertips.

Watts

2 = Two beats in a measure
4 = A quarter note gets one beat
BINGO
RUFF! Ruff!
There was a far - mer had a dog, and
Bing - o was his name oh, B - I - N - G - O
B - I - N - G - O and Bing - o was his name oh.
DO YOUR EARS HANG DOWN?
Do your ears hang down; do they wiggle to and
fro? Can you tie them in a knot? Can you tie them in a
bow? Can you toss them over your shoulder like a con ti nen tal
soldier do your ears hang low?

FOCUS: Bow technique. Use only a few inches of bow on the eighth notes and many inches on the quarter notes. Also keep your bow in the best spot and use just the right amount of pressure to maintain a clear sound. You have to test different spots and different pressure to see what sounds the best.

SERAGLIO

From an opera by Mozart

MY PONY
Watts
THE BLUE BELLS OF SCOTLAND

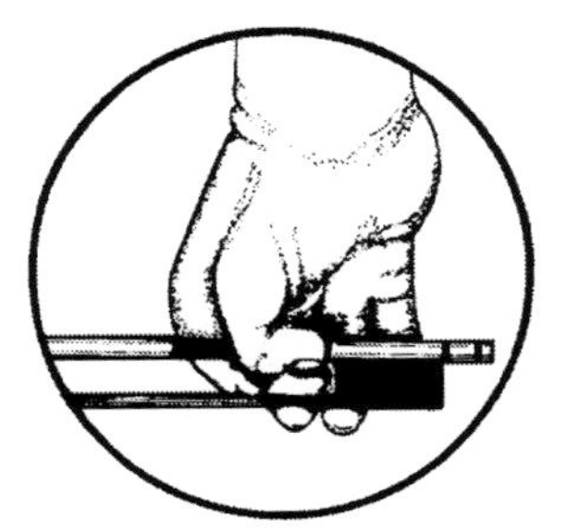

EXERCISE FOR BOW CONTROL & CELLO SOUND

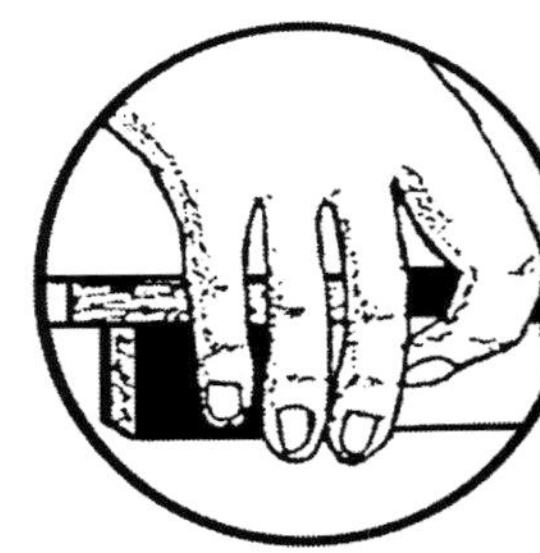

Use ½ of your bow for each note. Watch your hand and bow. Check to make sure your wrist is bending in and out to keep your bow straight.

Each ¼ note gets half a bow. It makes no difference if they are single or slurred. Since you are going slow, you need a half bow for each so they will sound beautiful.

Every note is down bow. Make a great big circle with your bow arm as you lift your bow off the string and come back around for the next note. Keep a solid bow grip.

Play 4 short bows on each note. Keep your arm as still as possible. Move the bow with your wrist and a little arm motion. Keep your arm as still as you can. Play them at the frog and then at the tip.

4 short bows at the frog
1 long bow all the way to the tip
4 short bows at the tip
1 long bow all the way to the Frog

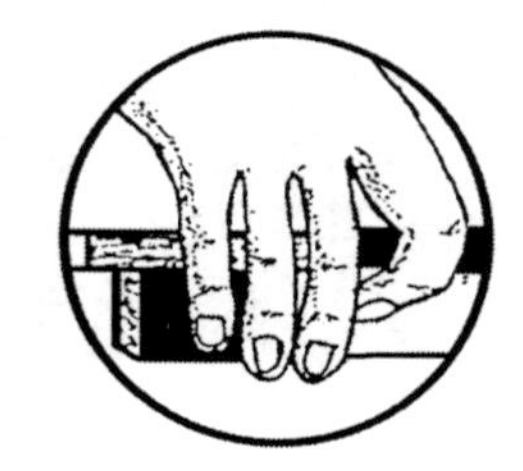

3 slurred, move your bow slowly
1 separate, move your bow fast
3 slurred, move your bow slowly
1 separate, move your bow fast

And the opposite goes:
1 separate move your bow fast
3 slurred move your bow slowly
1 separate move your bow fast
3 slurred move your bow slowly

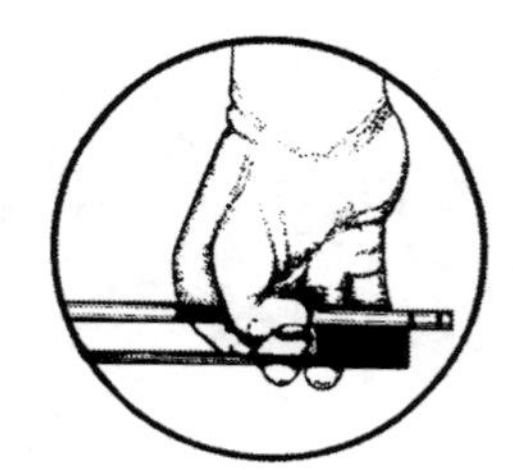

Make a smooth clear sound. Use lots of bow on the two quarter notes and very little on the eighth notes.

Use your whole of bow on the half note. Gently stop your bow between the two slurred quarter notes.

Another version is all quarter notes. Gently stop your bow between the 2 slurred. All the notes are exactly the same length.

Use very little bow on the 16th notes and play them fast. Use your wrist to move your bow on all the notes, not a stiff arm. Relax.

Try this one at the frog and at the tip. 2 eighth notes then 4 very fast 16th notes. Keep that wrist involved!

PIZZACATO

Put your thumb on the side of the fingerboard a few inches up from the bottom. You can pluck the strings with 1st, 2nd and 3rd fingers. Most cello players use just one finger unless they are playing many fast notes. We use our 1st or 2nd finger.

PIZACATTO BLUES

DAS BLUMCHEN WUNDERCHILE

POP GOES THE WEASEL

If you use your middle finger it is easier to hold your bow in.

PIZZACATTO

To play a chord, we strum the cello strings with our thumb just like a guitar player does. You can go one way, or back and forth. For classical music we always start with the bottom note.

STRUMMING WITH YOUR THUMB

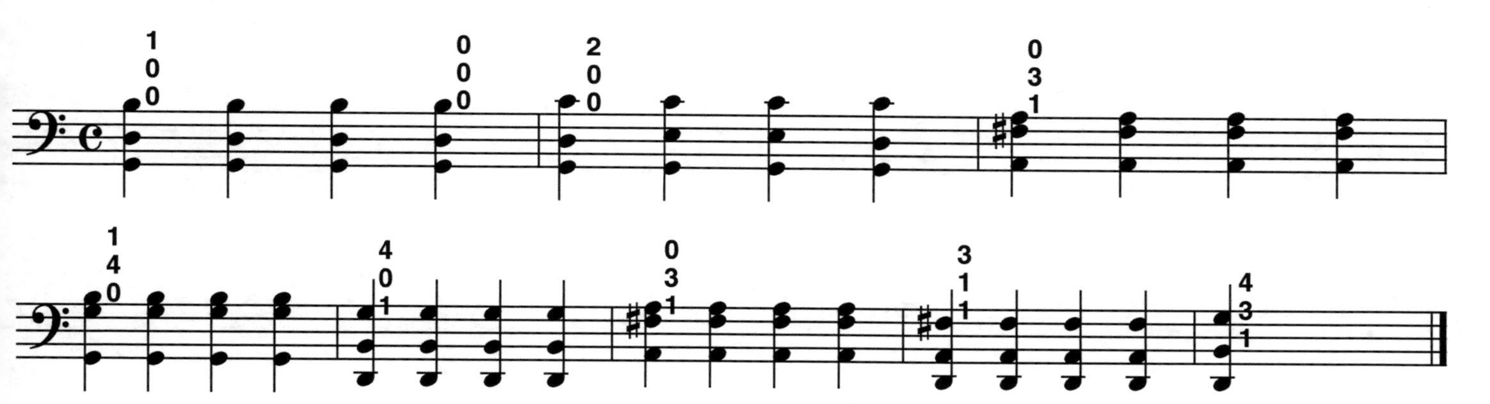

Remember: You have to lean harder on the lower strings to make a good quality sound.

FLEMISH SONG

Folk Song

DUET

Dotzauer

FREEDOM SONG
Broadly
Watts
f
2
1
f
0
4
2
0
4
p
cresc.
f
p
p
mf
f
rit.
ff

MUSETTE

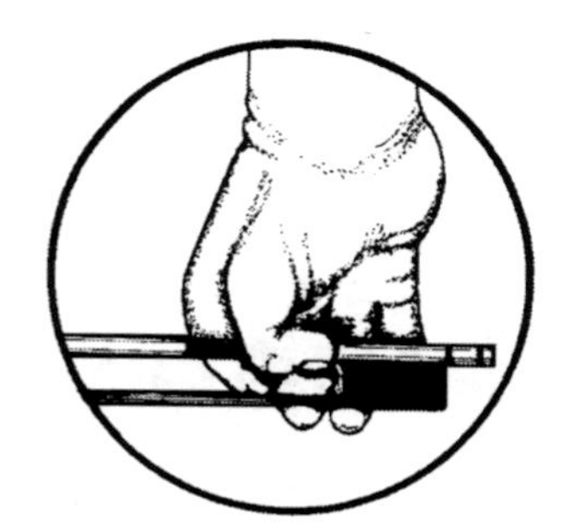

Use your whole bow on the down bow so you will have plenty of room for the 4 slurred.

Bach

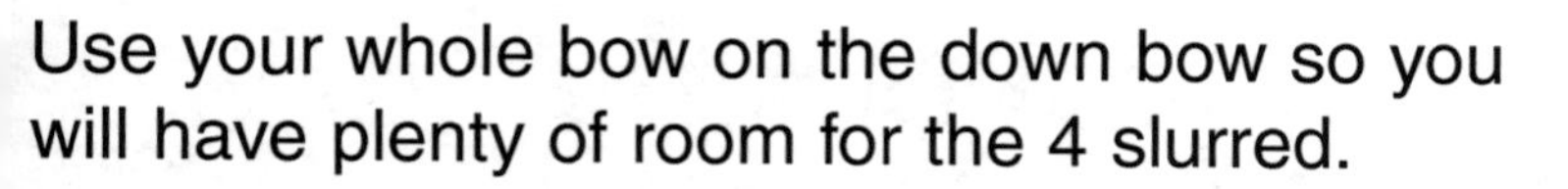

Make the G String Ring.

THE TIE

Sometimes you will see a curved line between two notes that are the same pitch. This is called a tie. It looks the same as a slur, but means play the two notes as one with no break in between.

BEAUTIFUL DREAMER

Really use your whole bow!

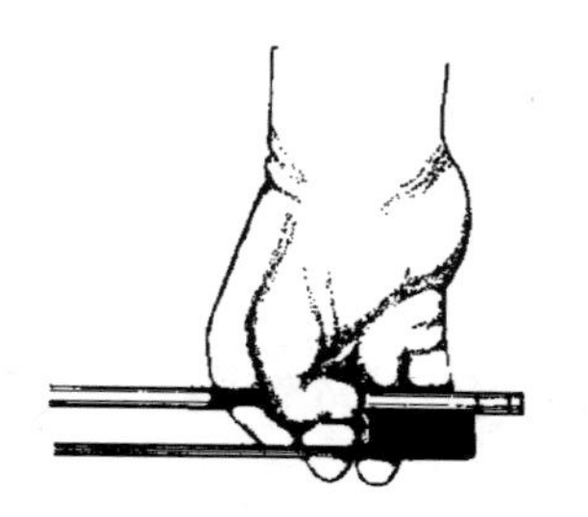

LAUGHING SONG
"Die Fleidermaus/ The Flight of the Mouse"
Johann Strauss Opera
Light and happy....
0
3
mf
THEME FROM BRAHM'S 1st SYMPHONY
Broadly, big beautiful bows
J. Brahms
mf
3

LEARNING TO BEAT YOUR FOOT TO THE MUSIC

First do the same note over and over so you can concentrate on coordinating your foot, your bow, your counting, and also of course making a beautiful sound.

Cellists beat time with their right foot, and here's how you can do it.

1. Get yourself in proper playing position.
2. Put the heel of your right foot on the ground and lift the front end poised to come down with the first down beat.
3. At the exact instant that your bow starts to play the first note your foot should hit the floor.
4. To beat time when a quarter note gets one beat; your foot should go down on the first half of the beat, and up on the second half.
5. Your foot goes down and up for each beat.
6. Since we count like this; one and two and three and four and......
7. We beat our foot the same way.
8. Toes down on ***one***; toes up on ***and*** (second half of the beat)
9. Toes down on two...... toes up on and.......

Practice on open string quarter notes first.
Down on one, up on and, down up on each note.

STRETCH POSITION FOR FLATS

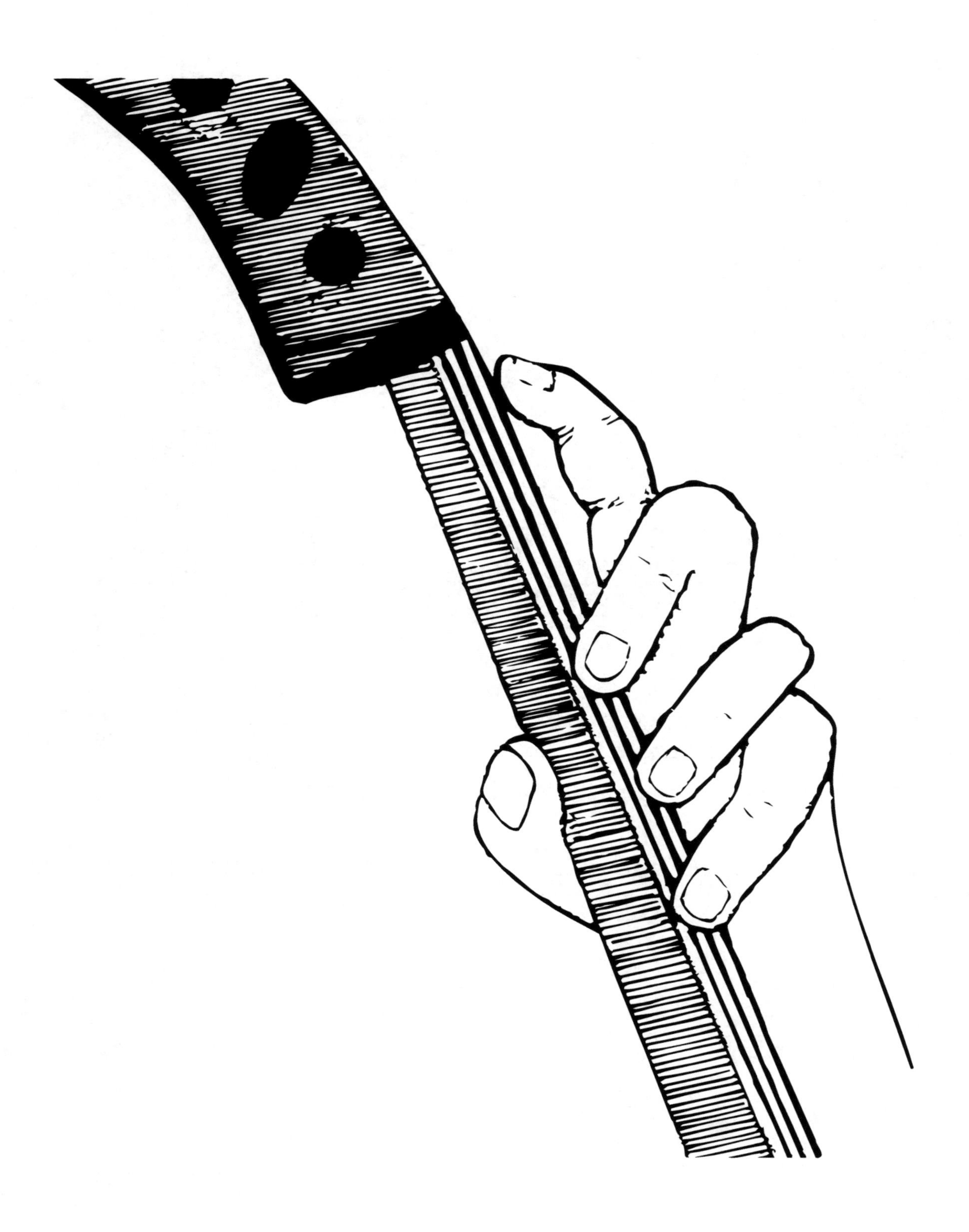

STRETCH POSITION FOR FLATS

Your first finger is the only one that moves.
The others including your thumb have to stay in place.

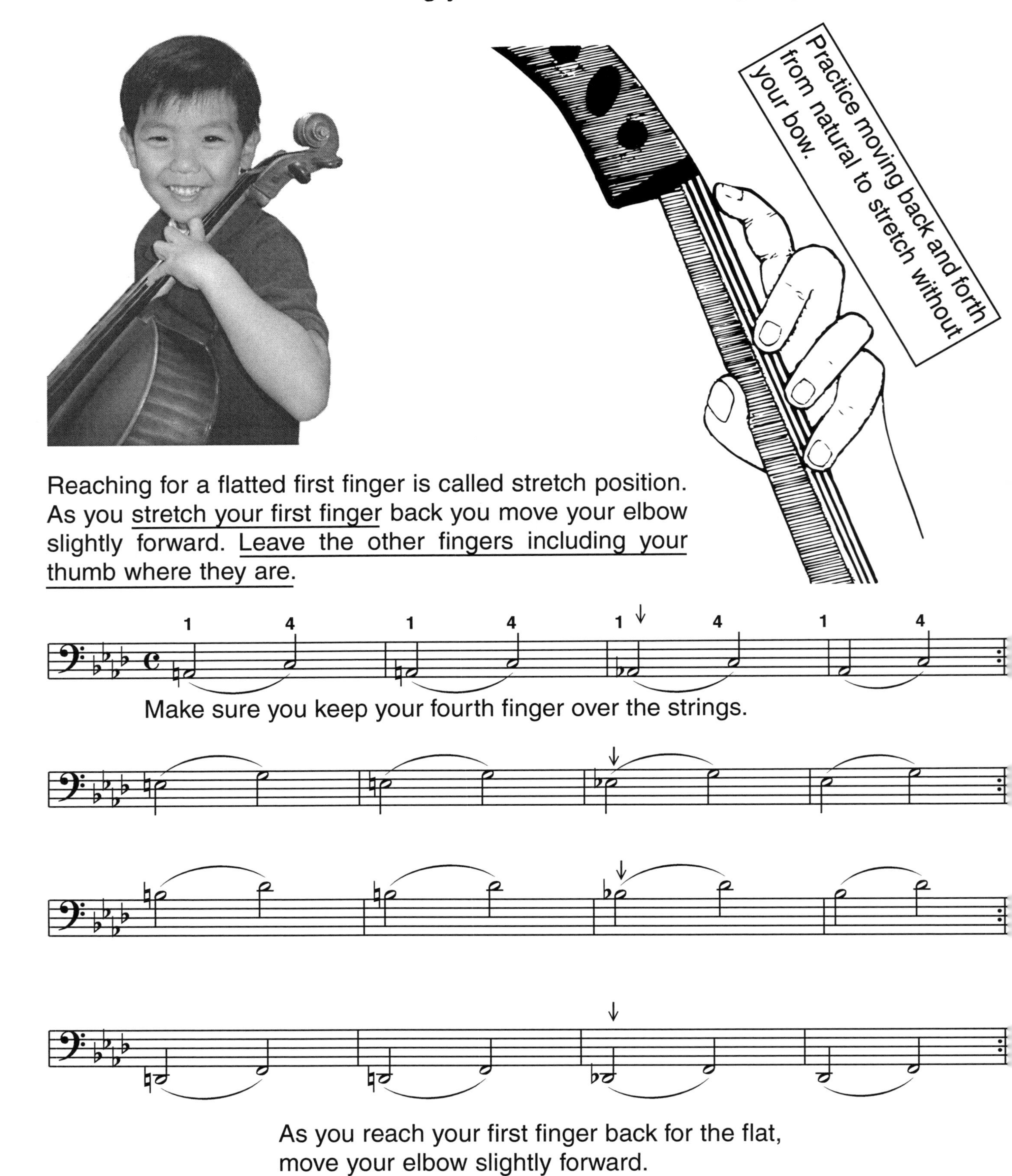

Reaching for a flatted first finger is called stretch position. As you stretch your first finger back you move your elbow slightly forward. Leave the other fingers including your thumb where they are.

Make sure you keep your fourth finger over the strings.

As you reach your first finger back for the flat, move your elbow slightly forward.

STRETCH FOR FLATS

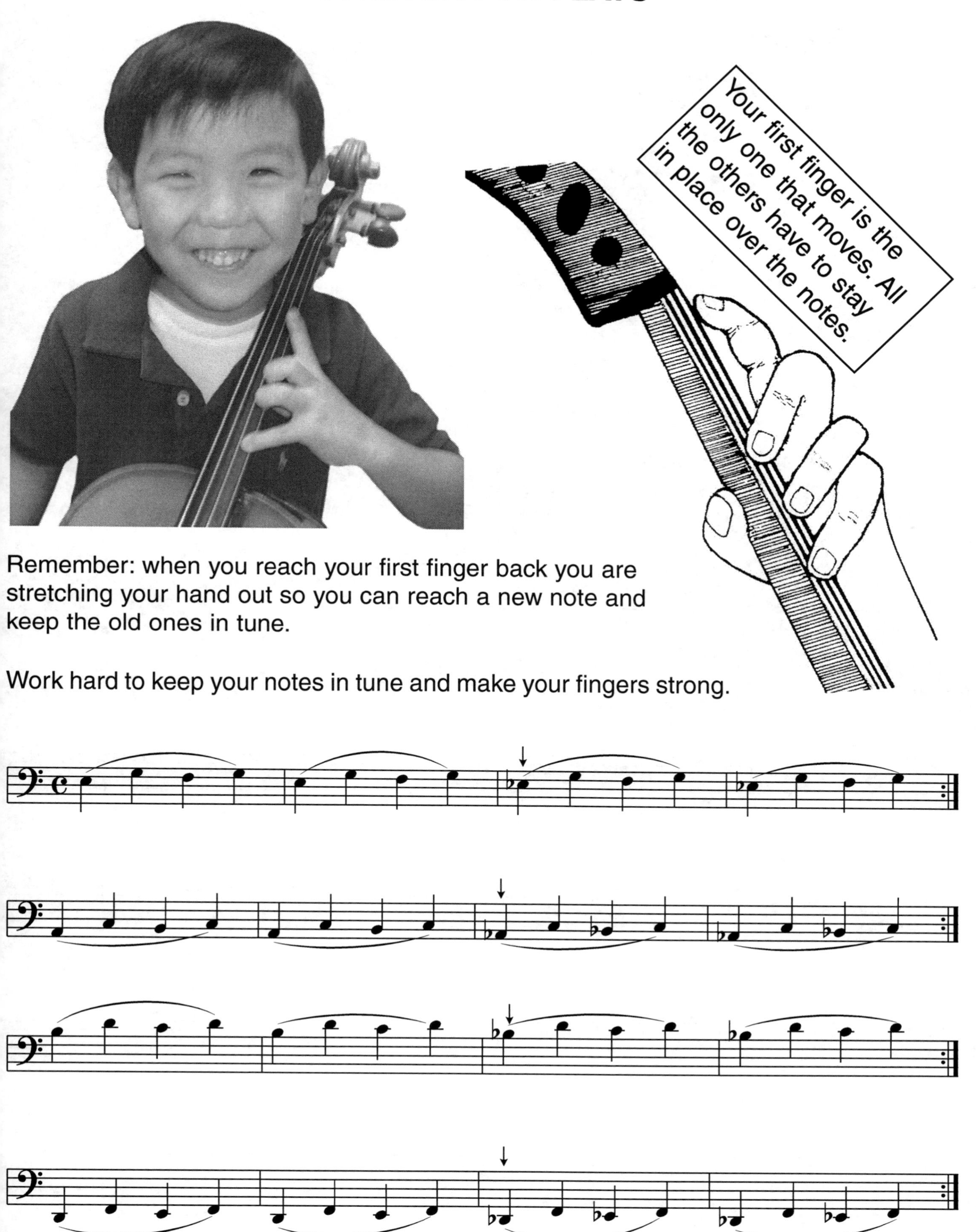

Remember: when you reach your first finger back you are stretching your hand out so you can reach a new note and keep the old ones in tune.

Work hard to keep your notes in tune and make your fingers strong.

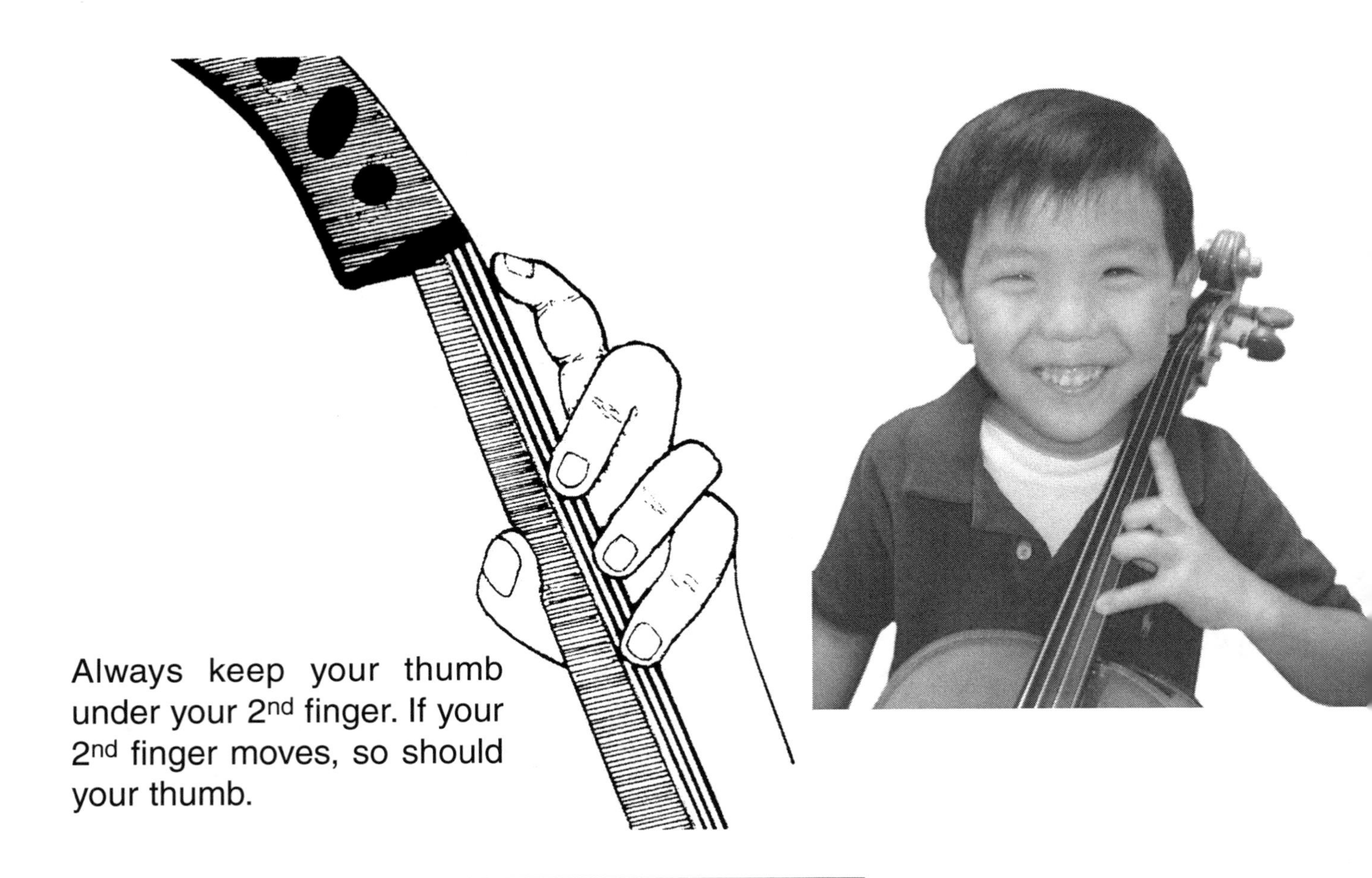

Always keep your thumb under your 2nd finger. If your 2nd finger moves, so should your thumb.

Before you play a note, put your hand in stretch position. Reach your first finger way back, don't move the others.

Arm away from the side of your body.
Make sure you repeat these exercises. It is very important to practice moving back and forth from stretch to natural positions.

Always reach only your first finger back keep the others in place.

TEDDY HAS BALLOONS

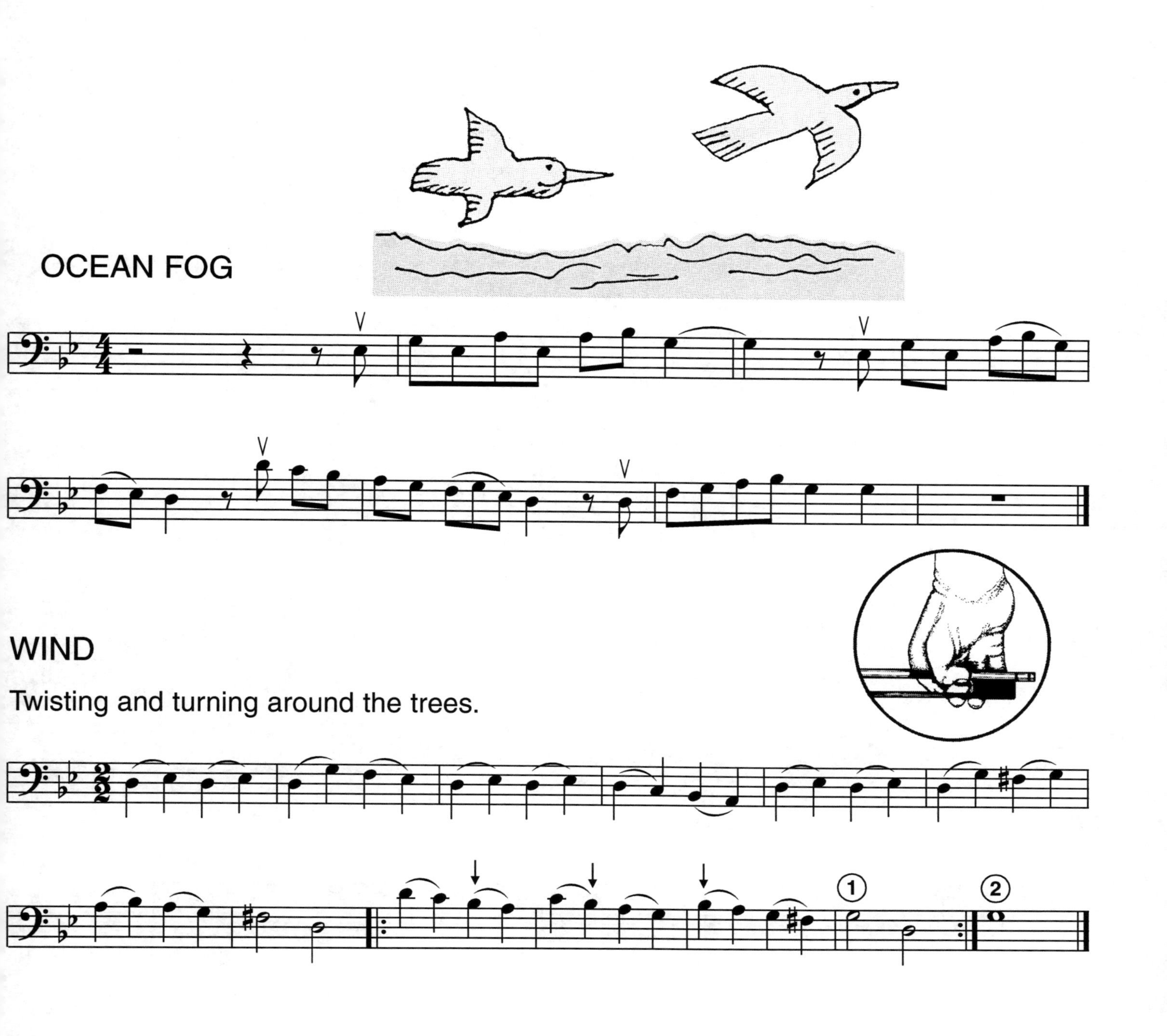

OCEAN FOG

WIND

Twisting and turning around the trees.

MONKEYS IN THE TREES

Use less than 6 inches of bow on each note. Keep a loose wrist.
Reach way back for the B♭. Keep your other fingers in place.

Kreutzer

FOCUS

Stretch your first finger almost straight back for the flatted note.

MINUET

STRETCH POSITION FOR SHARPS

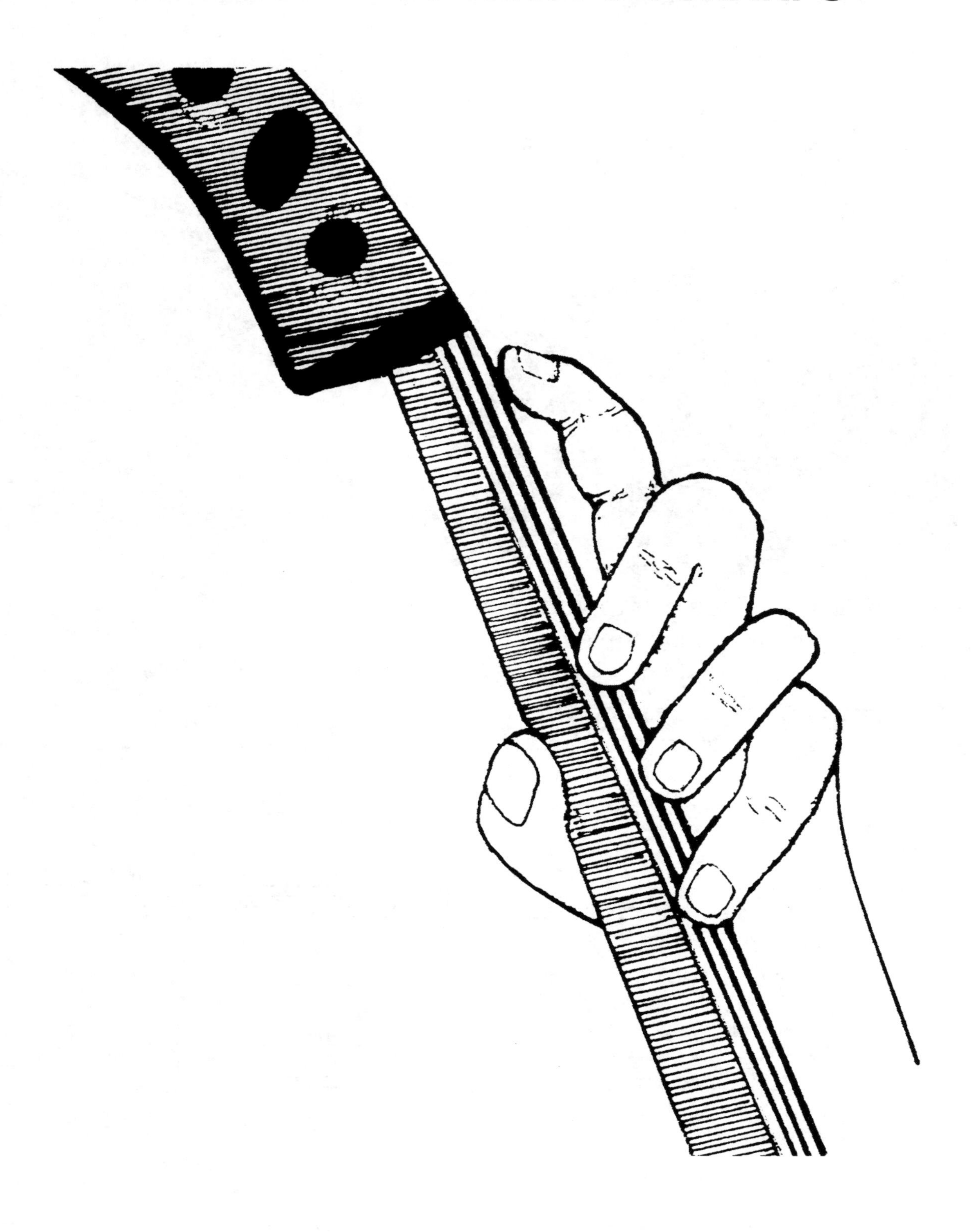

STRETCHING FOR SHARPS

When you put your 4th finger down, make sure all your others go down at exactly the same time.

MEMORIZE

In one smooth motion reach every finger but your first out one note and move your arm forward. Keep your thumb under your 2nd finger.

Each finger will have stretched out far enough to reach a new note but your first finger stays in the same spot.

Left arm up away from the side of your body! Don't forget, every finger BUT your first moves out to a new note.

When you look at this exercise, you can see that you will be starting in stretch position. Therefore you should get into stretch position before you start to play.
FOCUS: move your arm slightly forward and keep your thumb under your 2nd finger.

Keep all your fingers over the strings at all times.

Keep all four fingers over the strings at all times. When you finish a note lift your fingers straight up in the air, not back or to the side.

As you stretch your fingers out to play the new notes, move your arm forward just like you do to stretch for flats. Moving your arm forward makes stretching easier. Move everything in one smooth motion all at once.

STRETCH POSITION EXERCISE

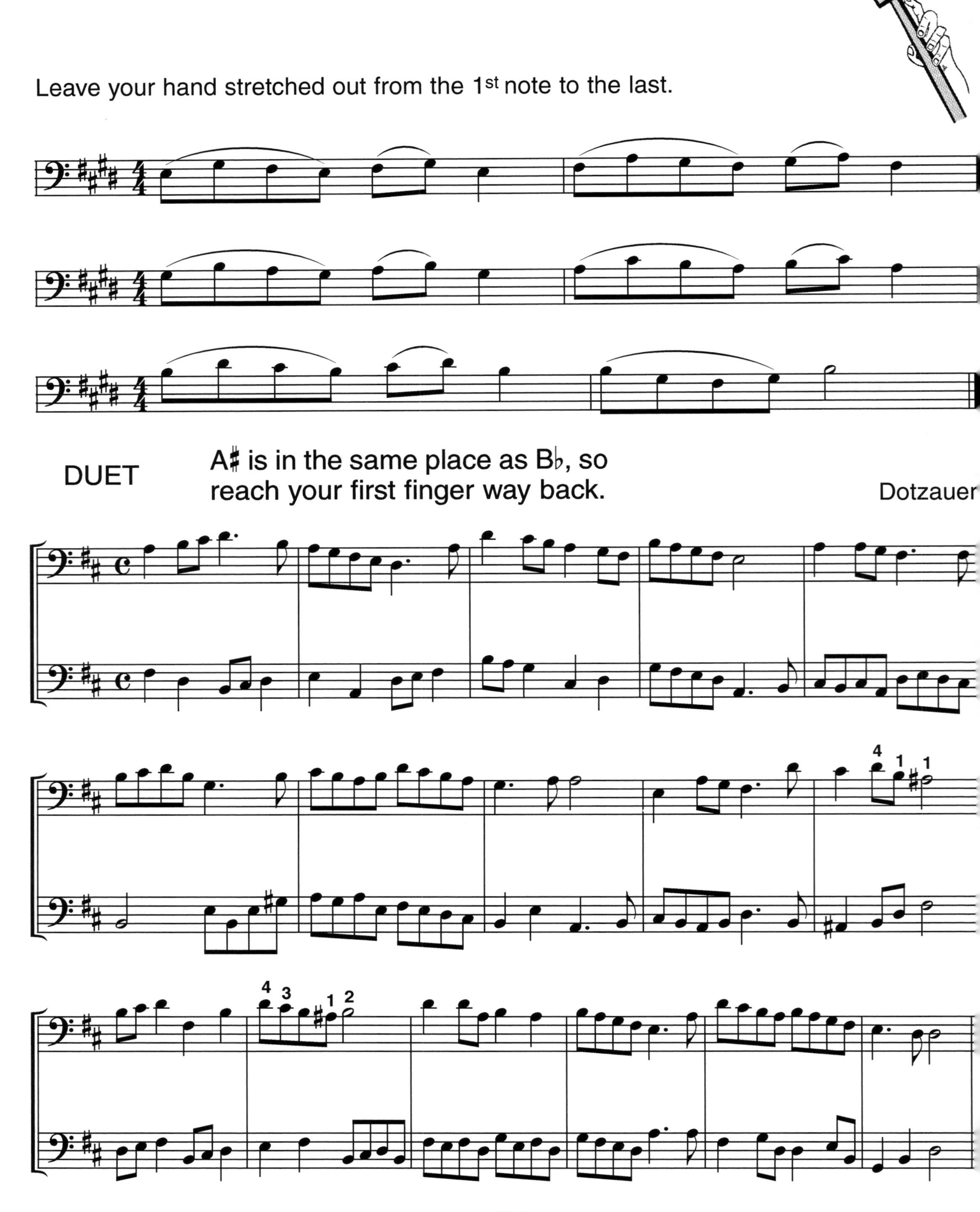

UP AND DOWN
Folk
1 2 4 0
3
CHINESE MELODY
Don't forget C# on the G string!
Folk
SWABIAN FOLK DANCE
½ position is (½ step) below 1st position. Every finger moves back one note.
Folk

REVIEW

Memorize the difference between stretch position for sharps and stretch position for flats.
THEY ARE THE OPPOSITE

FLATS

To stretch for flats move only your 1st finger straight back. Leave the others where they are. Move your arm slightly forward towards the cello.

To stretch for flats, leave everything in place move ONLY your 1st finger.

SHARPS

To stretch for sharps, you move all fingers up ½ step to play a new note. Keep your thumb under your 2nd finger and move your arm forward also.

To stretch for sharps, you move <u>everything</u> but your 1st finger.

STRETCHING FOR FLATS AND SHARPS TOGETHER

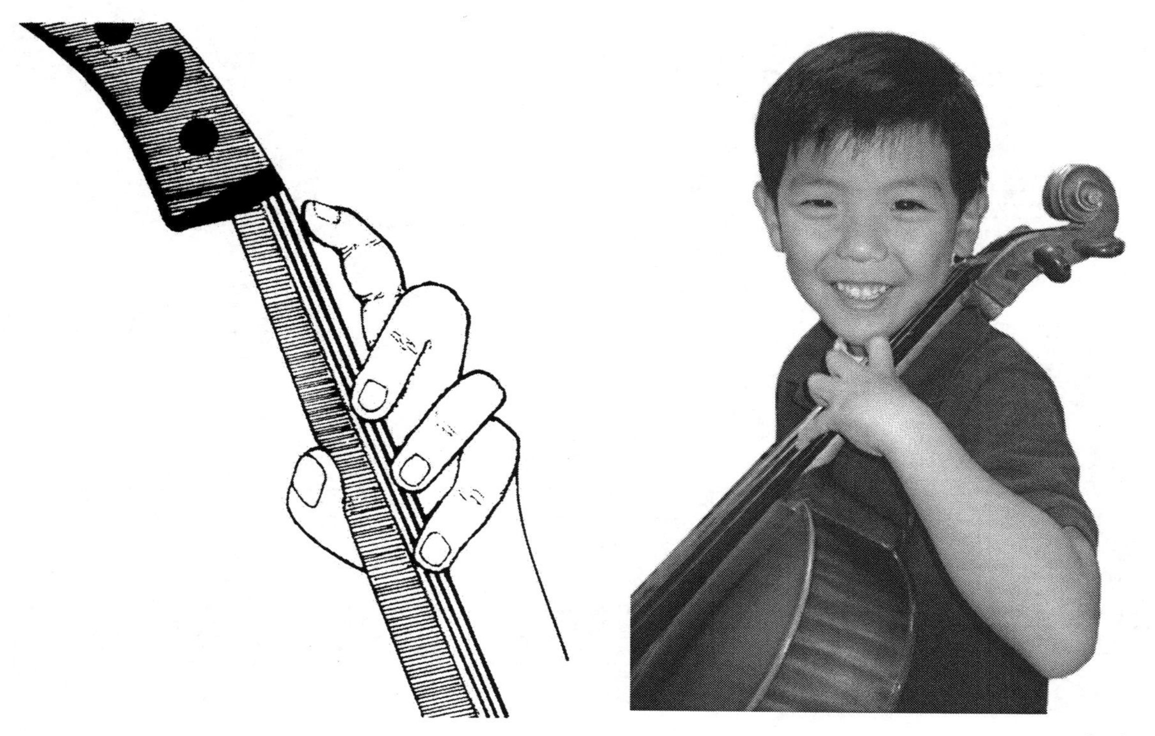

Orlando Cole

All 4 or 8 notes in a bow.

SHIFTING AND CHANGING POSITIONS
SEVICK SHIFTING OP 8

When shifting from one position to another, move everything at once. Keep your thumb under your hand, your arm straight and slide from the note you are playing to the next note in one smooth motion. Don't lift your finger off the string.

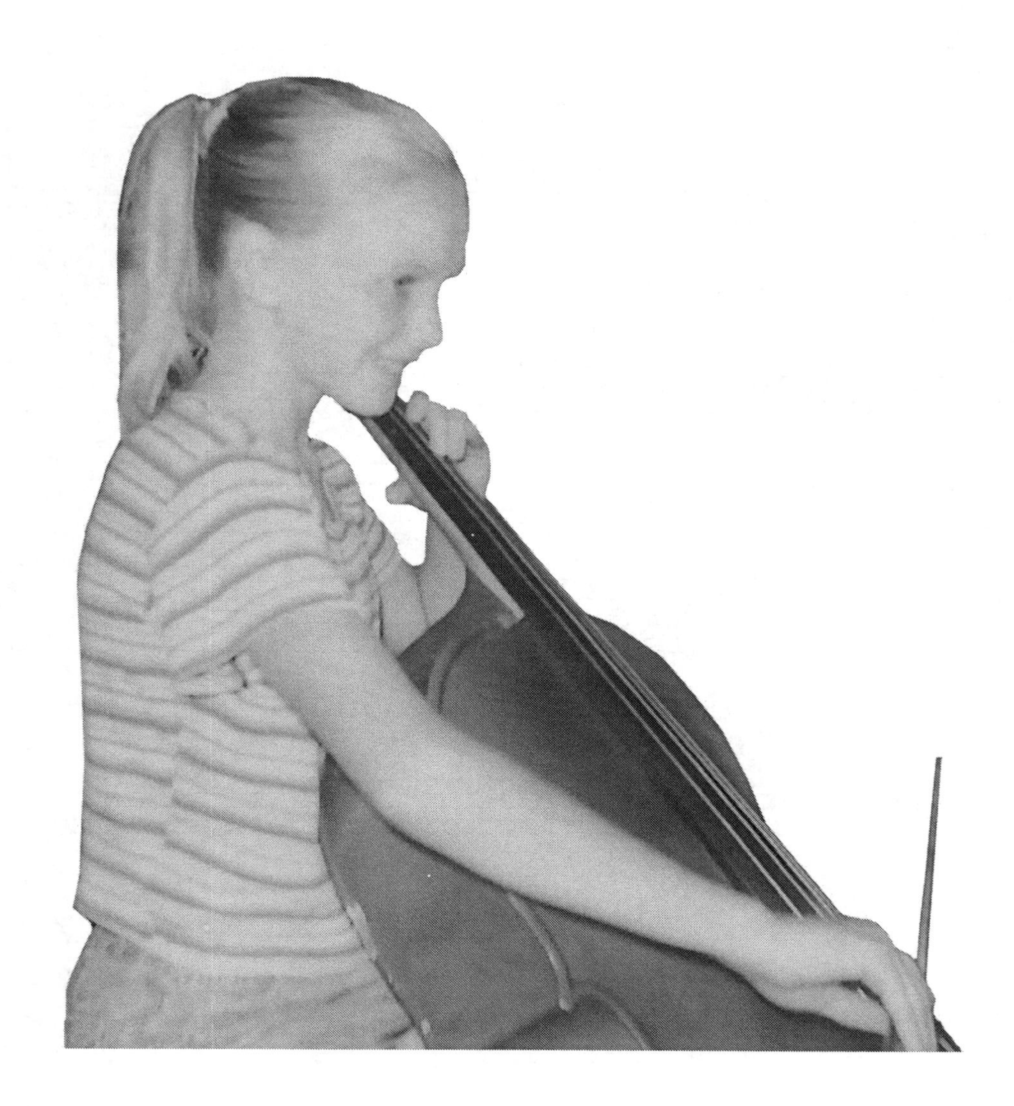

SMALL SHIFTS ON EVERY FINGER

Slide all your fingers including your thumb and
your whole arm all at once.

Metta Watts

SECOND POSITION

Even though 2nd position is very close to 1st, you must move your whole hand and arm to the new position.

THIRD POSITION

Your 1st finger goes where your 4th was. You can check your intonation with the open string.

FOURTH POSITION

Is easy to find. Put your thumb in the crook of the
cello's neck, and your 1st finger over top.

SLIDING TO 5TH POSITION HARMONIC

Keep your finger on the string.
Lift the pressure as you go.

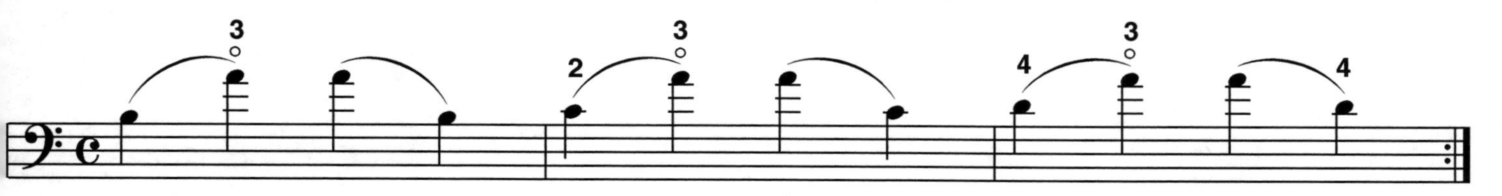

Play many times on every string
you must do a smooth accurate slide both ways.

MAJOR SCALES, ARPEGGIOS AND EXERCISES TO THREE FLATS AND SHARPS

C MAJOR has no sharps or flats

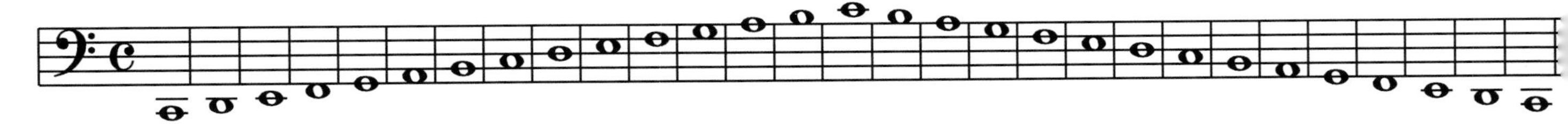

F MAJOR has 1 flat

G MAJOR has 1 sharp

B♭ MAJOR has 2 flats

D MAJOR has 2 sharps

E♭ MAJOR has 3 flats

A MAJOR has 3 sharps

C MAJOR SCALE

Has no sharps or flats

ARPEGGIO

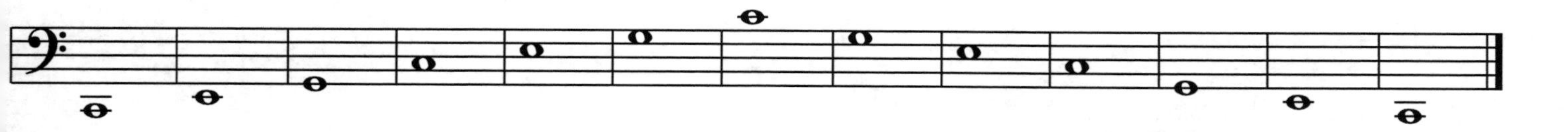

Orlando Cole

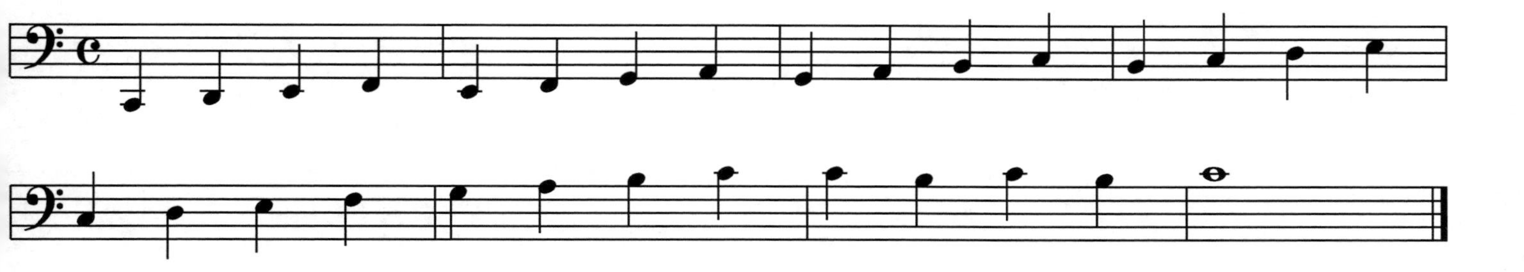

G MAJOR SCALE

Has one sharp

F♯

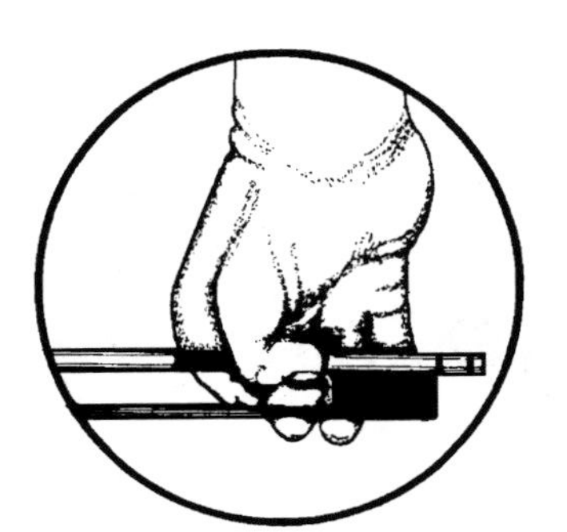

ARPEGGIO

Orlando Cole

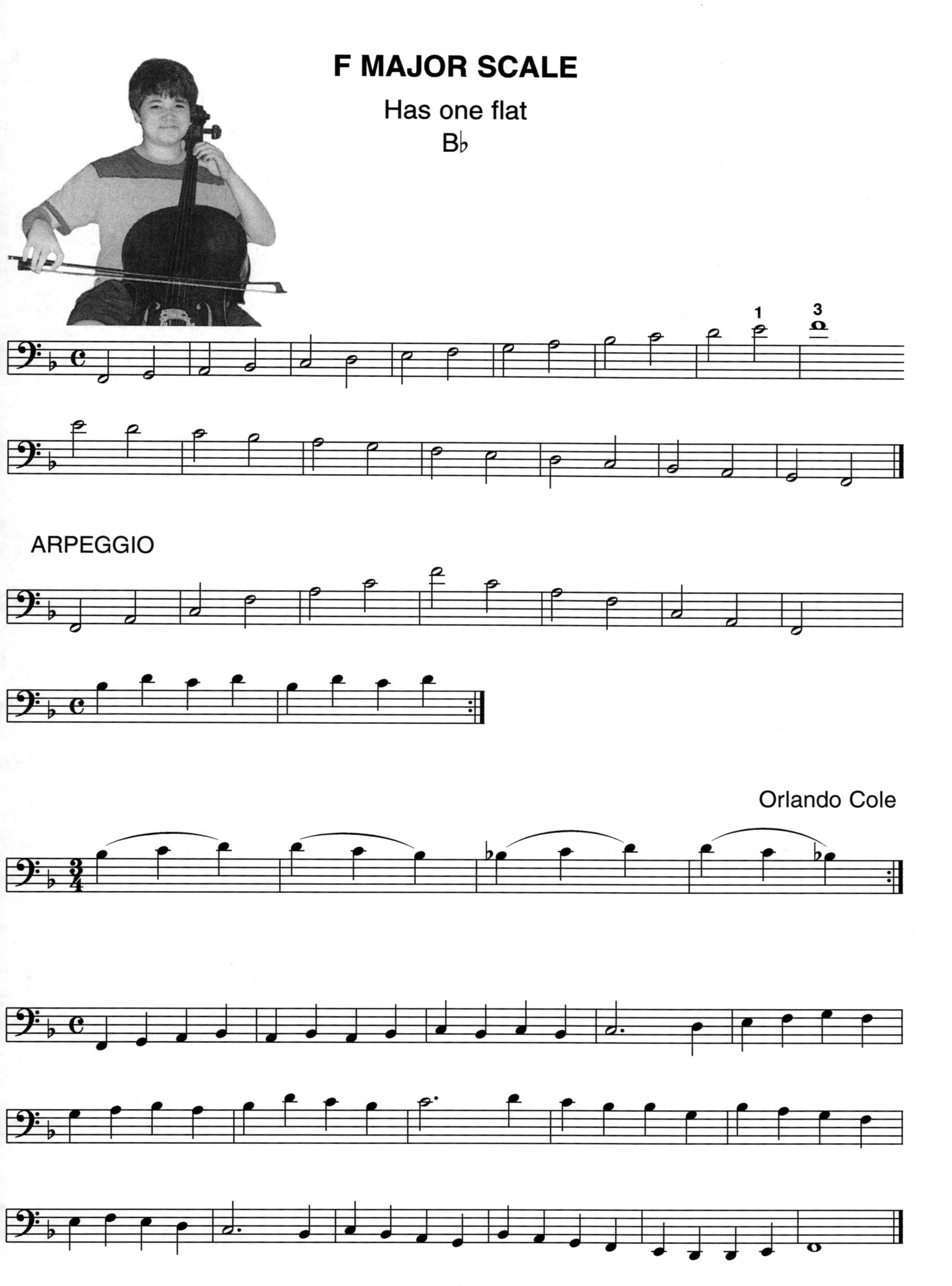
F MAJOR SCALE
Has one flat
B♭
1
3
ARPEGGIO
Orlando Cole

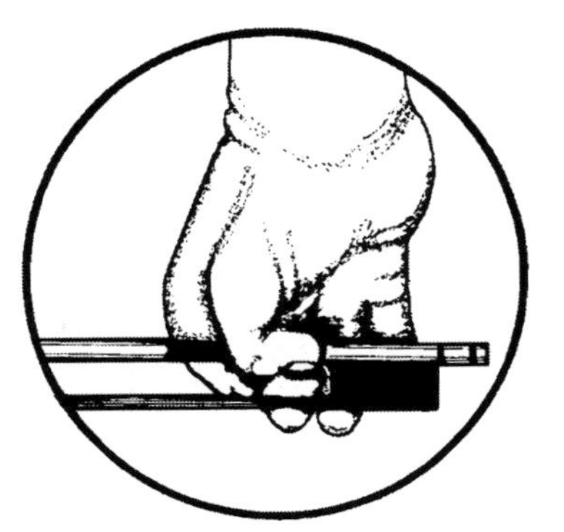

D MAJOR SCALE

Has two sharps
F♯ and C♯

ARPEGGIO

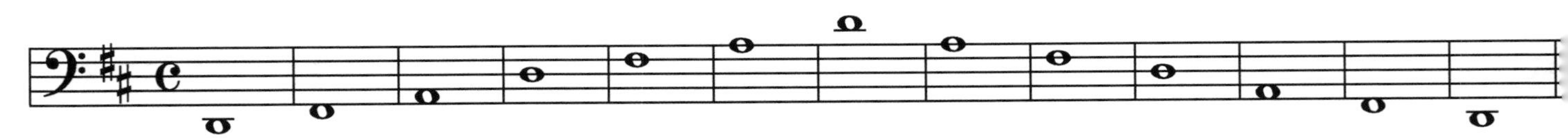

B♭ MAJOR SCALE

Has two flats
B♭ and E♭

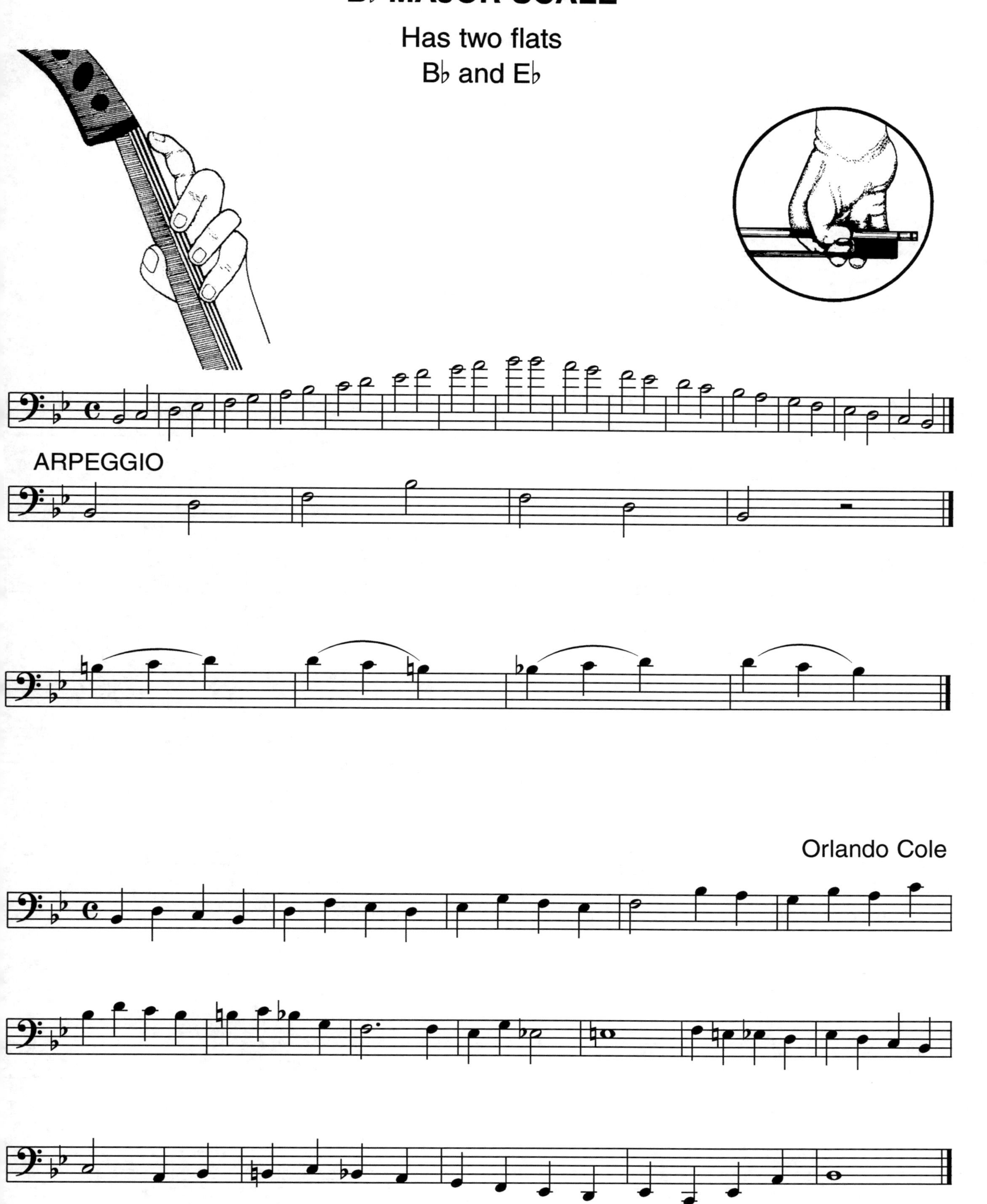

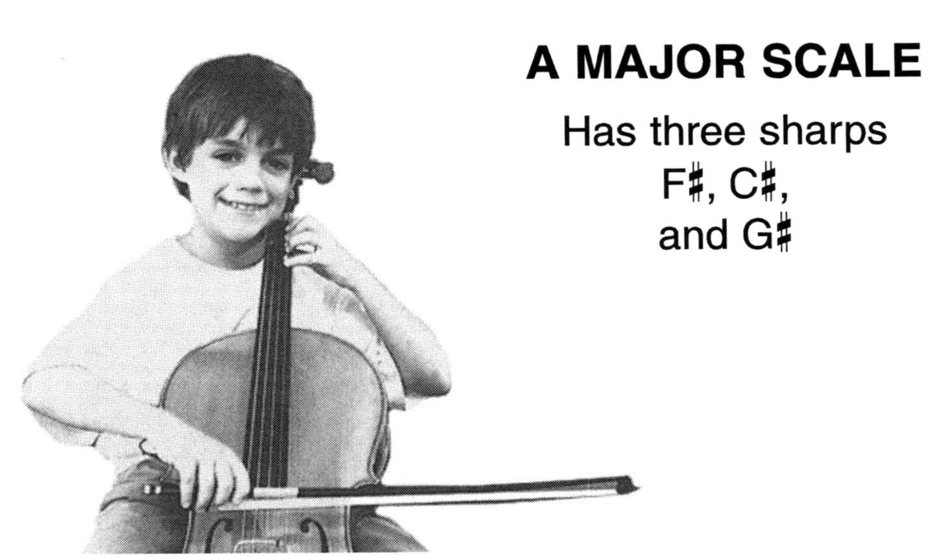

A MAJOR SCALE

Has three sharps
F♯, C♯,
and G♯

E♭ MAJOR SCALE

Has three flats
B♭, E♭,
and A♭

ARPEGGIO

Orlando Cole

HOLIDAY SONGS

HALLOWEEN
SPIRITS OF HALLOWEEN
pizz.
arco
arco
pizz.
arco
pizz.

JINGLE BELLS

GOOD KING WENSESLAS

WE WISH YOU A MERRY CHRISTMAS
O COME ALL YE FAITHFUL
0
3
p
f

JOLLY OLD ST. NICHOLAS

ANGELS WE HAVE HEARD ON HIGH

THE FIRST NOEL

UP ON A ROOF TOP

CONCERT PIECES

MINUET

J.S. Bach

HUNTERS CHORUS

C.M. Von Weber

THEME FROM ROSAMUNDE

Schubert

QUADRAILLE

THE MERRY WIDOW

Play with a vigorous happy bow stroke.

Schumann

CHORUS FROM "JUDAS MACCABAEUS"

Play with a big beautiful tone. Judas Maccabaeus should sound very dignified.

Handel

POLKA

Kuffner

CONTRA DANCE

PETITE GAVOTTE

Make sure your chords ring beautifully.

Lorenzetti

Certificate of Completion

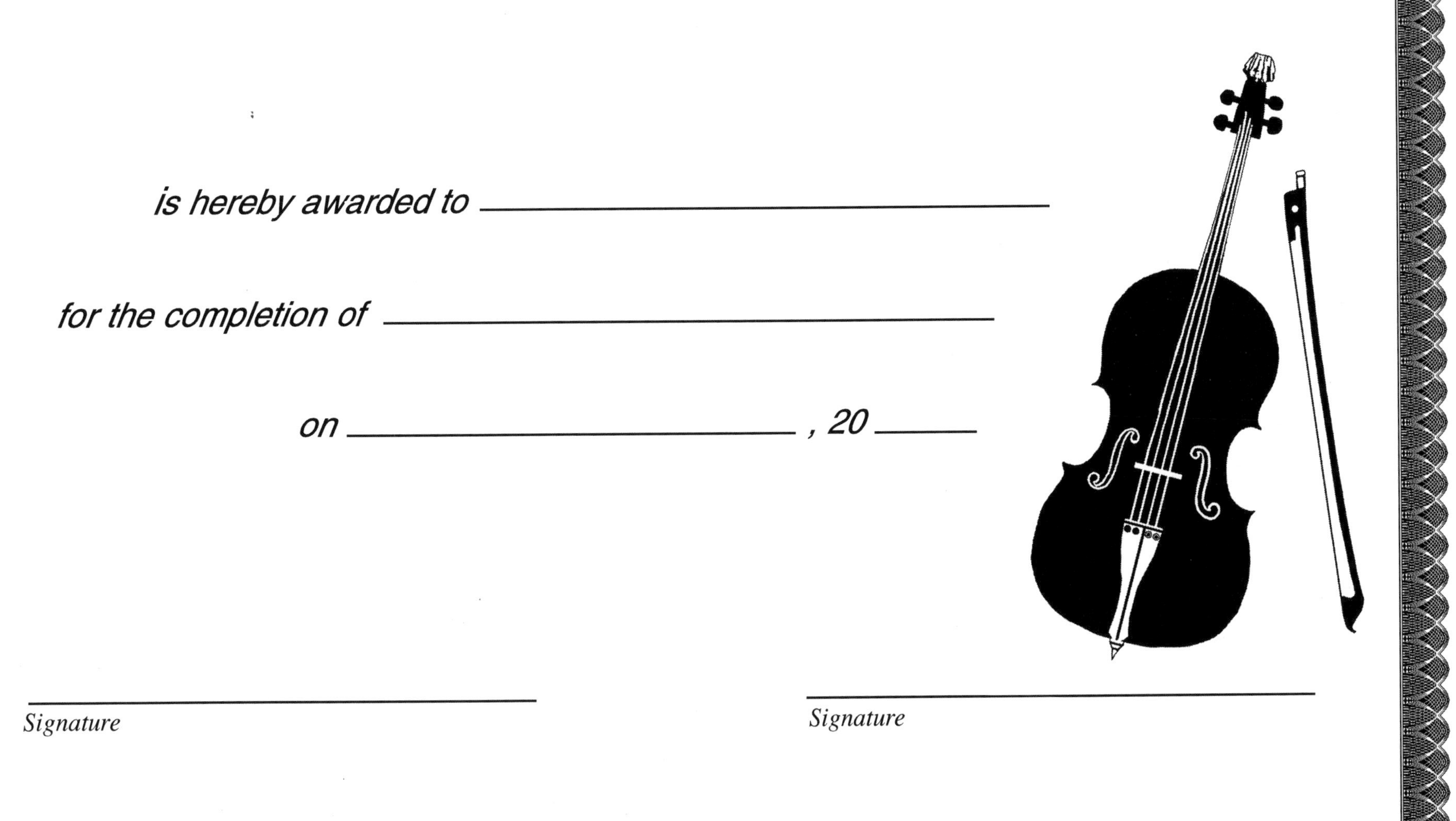

is hereby awarded to ______________________

for the completion of ______________________

on __________________ *, 20* ______

____
Signature

____
Signature

____
Date

____
Date